Cover: T. 'Prinses Irene,' one of the
most popular Triumph tulips, is
delightfully fragrant, forces easily,
and is a superb garden plant.
Its petals also taste good and
look pretty in a salad!

Page 1: Even T.,
'Lady Jane,' is a small, graceful,
species hybrid tulip, it is still at
home in a meadow planting.

Pages 2-3: A bold, colorful, large-flow-
ered, long-term perennial display can be
achieved by planting a group of
Darwinhybrid mixed tulips.

Pages 4-5: There are more T. 'Monte
Carlo' in the world than any other
tulip. Here, combined with a carpet of
Muscari armeniacum, it creates an
especially dramatic display.

Pages 6-7: T. 'Purple Prince', the color
of grape juice, shimmers in the early
morning sunlight.

Pages 8-9: The brilliant, gold-
feathered edges of the vivid red
T. 'Apeldoorn's Elite' attracts attention
even from a distance.

Tulips

FOR NORTH AMERICAN GARDENS

BY BRENT AND BECKY HEATH

b

bright sky press

albany, texas • new york, new york

bright sky press

Albany, Texas • New York, New York

Library of Congress Cataloging-in-Publication Data

Heath, Brent, 1945—
        Tulips for North American gardens / by Brent and Becky Heath.
            p. cm.
        Includes bibliographical references (p.).
        ISBN 0-9704729-6-X (hardcover : alk. paper)
1.Tulips—United States. 2. Tulips—Canada. I. Heath, Becky, 1945- II. Title.

SB413.T9 H43 2001
635.9'3432—dc21

                    2001037797

Book and Cover Design: Anne Masters Design, Inc.
Photography by Brent Heath
Project Management; Editorial Direction: Vivienne Jaffe
Distributed by: Sterling Publishing Co., Inc.
Printed in China through Asia Pacific Offset

Contents

Brent's Preface

My journey to discover the wonderfully diverse and charming world of tulips has been influenced largely by Dutch friends Carlos Van der Veek, Eric and Cees Breed, and Johann von Schapen. Carlos and I have studied together as fellow scholars, challenging each other to identify a tulip in bloom before we look at its label. Eric has introduced us to many growers and patiently tutored me, while Cees has one of the world's largest tulip collections, from which I have learned a great deal. Johann is the editor of the *Classified List and International Register of Tulip Names* as well as head of the committee that decides which new tulips are introduced and approves their names. He has been more than generous with his knowledge.

When I was a small boy growing up on our family daffodil farm in Virginia, my mother received a collection of tulips from our friend Matthew Zandbergen, a Dutch bulb grower, who thought mother should try mixing a few tulips among our daffodils. The types sent were mostly Kaufmanniana, Fosteriana, Darwinhybrid, and species. Those lucky, individual bulbs that escaped the voles brightened our gardens and added colors to the daffodils in my mother's flower bed for many years—a few descendants may even survive some 40 years later.

As an adult, I see tulips as an incredibly diverse group of plants whose brilliant, attention-getting flowers offer mood-enhancing decorations to enliven any occasion or celebration.

Opposite: Brent and Becky check tulip trials in one of their Gloucester, VA fields.

Brent OKs the quality of a field of T. 'Gudoshnik.'

Johann von Schapen discusses the merits of new tulip trials with Becky at the Tulip Registration Trial Gardens.

Opposite: John de Goede, our business manager in Holland and grower of very special bulbs, checks new tulips at KAVB Trial Garden.

Our daughter, Dorothy, home for spring vacation from college at peak tulip time said, "Daddy, I hope I won't upset you, but I really like tulips better than daffodils." So after generations as daffodil growers, our family has fully embraced tulips.

Becky's Preface

I am the middle child and only daughter in a wonderful, loving family. Vegetable gardens were always a large part of my parent's lives. In fact, I don't ever remember not having one. Of course, we all were expected to contribute to the planting, weeding, harvesting, and processing of the vegetables. Flowers, however, were an infrequent luxury. I don't remember being introduced to tulips until I married Brent.

Growers from around the world began to visit our farm in the early 80s to see our daffodil seedlings and the almost 3000 daffodil cultivars we grew at that time. At about the same time, our customers began to call us and say, "We already get all our daffodils from you . . . we'd like to get our tulips, crocus, and hyacinths from you as well." When we, in turn, visited growers we noticed the tulips and other bulbs they offered. We began to experiment with other bulbs here in our gardens. For me, that's when the love affair with tulips began.

It has been a real challenge for me to recognize tulips by sight without the help of a label or the tulip register, mostly because I am an auditory rather than a visual learner. Also, in recent years I have found it necessary to spend much more time in my office than out in our garden and trial fields. However, this has not kept me from appreciating the intricate detail of their beauty and the way in which tulips transform a garden!

Walking through tulip fields in The Netherlands each spring, checking on the crop, and always keeping an eye open for new and exciting developments, has forced me to be more attuned to tulips.

Planting them, admiring their beauty, and dealing with the challenges of not just growing them in our garden, but keeping them there, has turned me into a real tulip lover! Our oldest son, Jay, who has a degree in theater, said, "Mom, if something happens that I don't make it in the entertainment business, I think I could talk to customers about tulips. I think they're my favorite flower."

In the process of preparing this book, Brent and I have spent a great deal of time looking at tulips, taking pictures of them, and talking to the many commercial growers who produce millions of tulip bulbs. The diversity of North America's climate has raised our awareness of the wide range of gardening conditions that exist. Practical garden information is not a black-and-white issue, but dependent on many extenuating circumstances. We hope this book will add to your gardening success. Our aim has been to describe and picture only the cultivars that will be commercially available well into the future so that our information will remain current and helpful to you for a long time to come.

Opposite: Brent's "Kaleidoscope Garden"

Brent and Becky enjoying their flowers

I. *Introduction to Tulips*

Tulips are found in a multitude of sizes, shapes, and hues. They are splashed, striped, fringed, flamed, and feathered in contrasting combinations, filling spring with a blazing color parade. From their first appearance, their impact is tremendous, bringing joy to all who are privileged to be around them. Their amazing beauty almost takes one's breath away.

While the rose symbolizes love, romance, and happiness to Americans, tulips signify these qualities for the rest of the world and have done so throughout history. Persian mythology tells the story of a handsome young lad who, when rejected by a lovely young lady, cries copiously as he wanders aimlessly across the countryside. Wherever his tears touch the ground, tulips spring up as a token of his never-ending love. Another legend tells the story of Ferhad and Sirin. In order to marry Sirin, Ferhad first has to complete the task of bringing water from the other side of the mountain to the town — by tunneling through the mountain! When he is on the point of achieving this difficult feat, he learns of Sirin's death. Shocked, he swings his axe and inflicts a fatal wound on his own body. It is from Ferhad's blood that tulips grow.

Tulips could be considered the neon lights of the flower world, for surely their theatrical colors illuminate otherwise pale gardens emerging from winter doldrums or the subdued grays of masonry construction. Wherever tulips appear, they command the eye's attention.

A tulip's color, height, and bloom time differs according to variety choice, as well as the amount of light, heat, moisture, and minerals in the soil. Throughout the text we list average heights, colors, and bloom dates. However, unseasonable weather can alter these

Opposite: Lovely species T. turkestanica, *fragrant and multi-flowering, dates from 1875.*

Pages 16-17: You can almost see a full-spectrum rainbow in this display of Fringed and other tulips.

averages by as much as two to three weeks in blooming, 6-12" in height, and one to two shades in color intensity. Nature in all of its wonder and beauty is a variable feast.

Tulip Species and Wild Forms

Tulip bulbs that are wildflowers or occur in nature in parts of Asia and Europe are referred to as *species*. Wild, or species, tulips are frequently found in mountainous terrain, often in areas with cold, snowy winters, damp, moderate to warm springs, and hot, dry summers. The bulbs have been beautifully adapted: buried deeply they can endure a cold winter; they can emerge, grow quickly and bloom in spring when the weather is optimal; and then they shed their leaves and go dormant during the hot, dry summer. The bulb is truly one of nature's marvelous creations. Please limit your species purchases to those that have been nursery propagated and not collected in the wild so we can help preserve the colonies that still remain.

The Tulip Industry, Past and Present

Species, or wild tulips, discovered by Turkish explorers, grow in an area that stretches from Eastern Europe through the Middle East and the former Soviet Union to northern China. It is believed that the Turks began cultivating and refining wild tulips as early as 1000 A.D., making it one of the oldest ornamental plants continuously developed. The first glimpse of the tulip came from a 12th-century Bible in which tulip flower motifs were used to decorate the colorful letters of the headings. Poet and philosopher Omar Khayyám also mentions tulips in his writings in the 12th century.

Written and illustrated records of tulips were first encountered in Europe in the 1500s. Their early botanical name was 'lilionarcissus.' The word *tulipa* is believed to have originated with the Turkish word *tuliband* (turban) for the flower's resemblance to the traditional Turkish headdress. Later the word evolved to *tulipan* and then *tulipa*. A tulip is still a tulip whether the French call it *tulipe*, the Dutch *tulp*, the Germans *tulpe*, or the Spanish *tulipan*.

In 1554, it is said that Ogier Ghislain de Busbecq mentioned the tulips that bloomed in his Constantinople garden in his correspondence. By 1559, Conrad Gesner, a Swiss botanist, saw several tulips in a garden. Two years later his first botanical drawings of tulips

Hortus Bulborum in Leiden

appeared. Records indicate that botanist Carolus Clusius (1526-1609), while in Holland, received tulip bulbs, as well as other types of bulbous plants in 1571. This began the period known as the Renaissance of Horticultural Development, which saw the birth of the Dutch bulb industry. In 1580, Clusius sent tulip bulbs to England, spreading the excitement about this amazing bulb. Records indicate that in 1594 tulips first bloomed in Holland in the University of Leiden's *Hortus*, a small botanical garden. These tulip bulbs and seeds had been given to Clusius by the Austrian ambassador to the Ottoman Empire. *Hortus Botanicus* in Leiden, The Netherlands, is still open today where a recreation of Clusius' garden displays descendants of some of the original tulips. In Shakespeare's day, not much later, John Gerard's *Herball* (1597) describes seven sorts of tulips.

Tulip bulbs were sent to France in 1611 and by 1634 "Tulipomania" was in full bloom. It was to last only until 1639. English horticulturist John Parkinson included engravings of 140 varieties of tulips, which he called the *turks cap*, in his *Paradisi in Sole*

Paradisus Terrestris (A Choice Garden of All Sorts of Rarest Flowers, 1629).

Tulips became symbols of status as the Dutch enjoyed great wealth when their country was a great trading power. During *"tulipomania,"* special bulbs—especially the beautiful Rembrandt tulips—reached astronomical prices. At this time, speculation on something as elusive as the future development of a tulip bulb became known as the "wind trade" (prices made up out of thin air). Speculation on tulip bulbs during "tulipomania" seems to be similar to the turn of the 21st-century speculation in Internet businesses, both based on an unwarranted assumption of lasting value rather than reality.

"The Wind Trade," satire of the bulb trade during the peak of "Tulipomania."

Presently, the traditional bulb-growing area known as "de Bollendruk" (the Bulb District) is located in a narrow five- to 10-mile-wide strip on the sandy west coast of Holland just behind the sand dunes and bordering the dairy farms to the east. This area is located north of Leiden and south of the city of Haarlem, with many small towns surrounded and supported by the bulb industry. The most noted are Hillegom, where the Royal General Bulbgrower's Association (KAVB) is located; Lisse, where three major bulb auction houses handle the majority of the wholesale transactions between the growers and the brokers; and Sassenheim and Noordwijk to the south. Tulip production is increasing in the northwest corner of Holland (the province of North Holland) around Petten, Breezad, and Anna Paulona. The province of Freezeland produces many tulip bulbs, primarily for the forcing trade. We would be remiss if we didn't mention that England, the U.S., France, Japan, Chile, South Africa, and New Zealand also devote substantial acreage to producing tulip bulbs.

Here in North America, historical evidence shows tulip bulbs were brought along with other dear, non-essential household possessions by early settlers who wanted something of their treasured home gardens in the new land. There are also many accounts of orders from "back home" for essentials that included a few tulip bulbs to make life brighter. Much early American floral art shows arrangements with tulips, evidence of their importance in our life as a young nation, and of our ties to the past.

A Word About Heirloom Tulips

The term "heirloom" means different things to different people. Some interpret it as having the same meaning as "antique" and, therefore, objects 50 years old meet the required criterion. In that case, all tulips introduced before 1951 would be considered "heirloom." Others think this rule is not strict enough and insist that 100 years be the criterion. Still others use the word "heirloom" loosely to define bulbs that are appropriate to the year when their particular garden was established. In any case, reliable catalogues and garden centers list information about "old" tulips, giving the dates of introduction, so you can determine if the cultivars that appeal to you suit your site.

Many historic houses that have become museums or public attractions used journals and writings of the previous owners to determine what might have been planted originally in the gardens. If information was not available for a particular garden, horticultural journals written during the same time period, listing plants that were used in other gardens in the same region, became the basis on which plant selections were made. For instance, Thomas Jefferson kept very specific records of what he planted in his garden at Monticello. Some of the old cultivars are no longer available and some of the species names have changed. The drawings and illustrations in Curtis' *Botanical Magazine*, Gerard's *Herball* and other garden-oriented publications of the time have been helpful in matching old types with revised nomenclature.

One interested in planting an 18th-century garden can learn a great deal by visiting one of the lovely, historic homes. Gardens of historical value that we've visited (and that have used our bulbs) are: Gunston Hall, Lorton, VA; Mount Vernon, Mount Vernon, VA; Tryon Place, New Bern, NC; Biltmore Estates, Asheville, NC;

Tulip field in the south of Holland with an old-fashioned windmill

Tulip field in the north of Holland with a modern windmill

Plant an Heirloom

Many tulip bulbs classified as "heirloom" are species types and often naturalize when they are planted in their "happy spot" and are not bothered or eaten. Non-species often perennialize, or repeat bloom, year after year like a perennial. Some commercially available 50-year-old or older tulips are:

T. albertii 1877, *T. altaica* 1825, *T.* 'Apeldoorn' 1951, *T.* 'Attila' 1945, *T. biflora* 1776, *T.* 'Black Parrot' 1937, *T.* 'Blue Parrot' 1935, *T.* 'China Pink' 1944, *T. clusiana* var. *chrysantha* 1948, *T.* 'Couleur Cardinal' 1845, *T.* 'Cum Laude' 1944, *T.* 'Dreaming Maid' *1934*, *T.* 'Fantasy' 1910, *T.* 'Generaal de Wet' 1904, *T. hageri* 'Splendens' 1945, *T. humilis* 1844, *T.* 'Johann Strauss' 1938, *T. kolpakowskiana* 1877, *T.* 'Lilac Perfection' 1951, *T. linifolia* 1884, *T.* 'Madame Lefeber' 1931, *T.* 'Maureen' 1950, *T.* 'Maytime' 1942, *T.* 'Maywonder' 1951, *T. maximowiczii* 1889, *T.* 'Mount Tacoma' 1924, *T.* 'Mrs. John T. Scheepers' 1930, *T.* 'Oxford' 1945, *T.* 'Peach Blossom' 1890, *T.* 'Picture' 1949, *T. polychroma* 1885, *T. praestans* 'Fusilier' 1939, *T.* 'Prinses Irene' 1949, *T.* 'Purissima' 1943, *T.* 'Queen of Night' 1944, *T.* 'Renown' 1949, *T. tarda* 1933, *T. turkestanica* 1875, *T.* 'Uncle Tom' 1939, *T. urumiensis* 1932, *T.* 'West Point' 1943, *T.* 'White Parrot' 1943, *T. wilsoniana* 1902, *T.* 'Wirosa' 1949.

Dumbarton Oaks, Washington, DC; Agecroft and The Virginia House, Richmond, VA; Independence Park, Philadelphia, PA; Pennsbury Manor, Pennsbury, PA; Sterling Forest Garden, Historic Hudson, NY; and Stan Hewyett Hall, Akron, OH. Colonial Williamsburg in Williamsburg, VA, is an entire village that not only has gardens, but also depicts in detail the lifestyle of colonial times.

Tulip Statistics

The tulip is one of the most popular flowering bulbs, with more than 10,000 hectares (25,000 acres) in production worldwide at the time of this writing. Approximately 125 species tulips have been found in the wild and more than 2,300 cultivars have been registered with the Royal General Bulbgrowers Association in The Netherlands, which is the worldwide authority for registering new tulip cultivars. Approximately 800 to 1,000 cultivars, species, and varieties of tulips are in general commerce today, with about 80% produced in The Netherlands. The majority (about 90%) are grown for forcing and for cut flowers, which means about 900 million blossoms are produced in greenhouses in The Netherlands and around the world annually. The rest are exported as bulbs for planting in gardens such as ours.

Benjamin Powell Garden in Colonial Williamsburg, VA

Opposite: Tulips displayed in the gardens at the Biltmore Estate in Asheville, NC

II. *Tulip Anatomy*

The genus Tulipa is a monocotyledon (one seed leaf) of the Liliaceae family. The major center of origin is from Eastern Europe to Central Asia and China. Tulips are classified as true bulbs and possess anywhere from two to six concentric fleshy scales similar in structure to the daffodil bulb. The scales are attached to a basal plate located at the base of the bulb. During growth season, roots emerge from the basal plate on the outside, and flower and leaf buds on the inside.

A true bulb is essentially a large bud surrounded by swollen leaf bases that resemble the connective scales on an onion. These scales have adapted to store food during dormancy and in difficult growing times during the year.

A thin, dry, brown papery skin called a tunic protects the bulb. It is considered a visible sign of good health when one is selecting bulbs from a bin at a garden center. When bulbs are received by mail order, however, the tunics are often broken away or cracked. This is not a problem, unless rough handling has bruised the bulbs. In that case, they will exhibit brown and white lesions (scars) on the bulb. Each bulb should be checked carefully and discarded if the lesions appear to be spreading. Small nicks and blemishes are generally not a problem.

Tulip bulbs begin to initiate roots in the fall when the soil temperature is 60°F or less at root level and adequate soil and moisture signal the bulbs that it is time to renew the process of annual growth. Tulips take up moisture and nutrients as soon as roots form and continue to do so in most climates, unless the ground is frozen, until the leaves die in early summer. During the winter, the flower slowly begins to mature. Then, as the weather begins to warm, the flower bud and surrounding leaves begin to emerge from the bulb, waiting for the right combination of warmth and proper day length to probe upward through the soil surface and bloom. The bloom triggers new growth points in the mother bulb that will be the next year's bulbs

Above: Healthy tulip bulbs in all sizes
Below: Fusarium lesions on tulip bulbs

Opposite: Sharing similar color and complementing each other's strengths, Lily-Flowering T. 'Marilyn' and Triumph T. 'The Mounties' make an eye-catching combination.

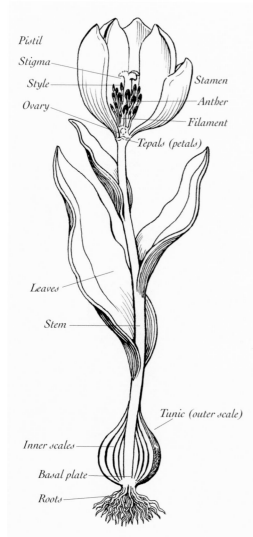

Pistil
Stigma
Style
Ovary
Stamen
Anther
Filament
Tepals (petals)

Leaves

Stem

Tunic (outer scale)

Inner scales

Basal plate

Roots

Root

Basal plate—the bottom portion of the bulb from which the roots emerge

Bulb

Inner scales—energy storage unit

Tunic—protective covering of bulb

Stem

Leaves

Flower

    Tepals—indistinguishable petals and sepals of a flower

    Pistil—female reproductive structure

        Stigma—the tip of the pistil that receives the pollen

        Style—the portion of the pistil connecting stigma and ovary

        Ovary—the swollen basal portion of the pistil containing the ovules that, after fertilization, become the fruit containing the seeds

    Stamen—male reproductive structure, one of the six pollen-bearing organs

        Anther—the terminal pollen-bearing part of the stamen

        Filament—the thin stalk of the stamen that supports the anther

and blooms. After the spent flower and seed pod are removed (*see section on Deadheading*), all of the energy produced by photosynthesis in the leaves is stored in the new bulbs as starches to provide energy for next year's blooms. As the weather turns warm, the leaves mature (turn yellow) and the old bulb is transformed, leaving one or more "daughter" bulbs to begin the process all over again. The larger (at least 12cm) bulbs are blooming size, while smaller bulbs can become your planting stock. When they grow to 12cm or larger, they will be ready to bloom.

Most blooming-size bulbs produce two or more growth points. One of these buds will produce a flower or flowers, and the others will produce the daughter (or new) bulbs, which should bloom in subsequent years after sufficient growth.

The flower is made up of three sepals on the outside and three petals on the inside surrounding a superior, or tricarpellate, ovary and two whorls of three pollen-bearing stamens. The ovary can contain as many as 300 flat, black, triangular paper-thin seeds.

Tulip roots, unlike some other bulbs, are non-contractile, meaning they do not pull themselves deeper into the soil. Tulip roots are also non-branching, fairly brittle, and do not have root hairs. For these reasons, it is very important to plant the bulbs deeply enough in soil that their roots can easily permeate, and then not to disturb the roots once they have formed.

Divisions of Tulips

The divisions of tulips were recently reorganized by the KAVB (Royal General Bulbgrower's Association), which released the new tulip register in 1996. An explanation and list of the divisions according to the new register are in italics. Our own thoughts and findings follow each individual group description.

Single Early

Single-flowered cultivars, mainly short-stemmed and early flowering. Single Early tulips are among the oldest group of hybrid tulips. This group includes some of the oldest hybrids still in cultivation. Because Single Early tulips bloom early, they seem to be better equipped to withstand the strong winds and fluctuating temperatures of spring, and the flowers tend to last longer in the cooler temperatures. Several members of this group have proven to be long-term perennial tulips in our Tidewater, Virginia (zone 7) garden. Because of their moderate height and naturally early bloom time, they force well and are excellent for use in pots and containers. Many Single Early tulips have a sweet, musky fragrance that enhances their value, not only as cut flowers and potted plants, but also as garden plants. These tulips are wonderful for combination plantings with other spring flowering bulbs such as early and midseason daffodils, hyacinths, other early tulips (Fosteriana, Kaufmanniana, Triumphs, and species tulips), *Muscari*, Christmas Pearl, Chionodoxa, *Puschkinia*, and *Scilla siberica*.

They also are lovely in combination with perennials, biannuals, annuals, trees, and shrubs.

Double Early

Double-flowered cultivars, mainly short-stemmed and early flowering. They are sports (mutations) or hybrids of Single Early tulips and hence share similar characteristics, habits, and uses. These flowers are usually semi-double to double with most being in the shape of a peony or rose. They happily share garden space with similar plants and are especially well-adapted for use in patio planters and window boxes and are exceptional for forcing.

Triumph

Single-flowered cultivars, stem of medium length, midseason flowering. Originally the result of hybridization between cultivars of the Single Early Group and the Single Late Group. There are also some multi-flowered types and the heights vary from short to tall. Triumph tulips are among the most popular, widely grown, and hybridized (primarily in Holland) groups of tulips today. The main reason for their popularity is that they are great for forcing and pot culture, as well as seasonal bedding color. We have found that many bloom from midseason to late midseason. Since demand for forced tulips is high, growers seek to create new cultivars, and there are now more cultivars of Triumphs than any other type. These tulips have been bred to have a virtual rainbow of colors, strong, sturdy stems (generally short to medium height), and long-lasting flowers. A few individual cultivars fit the category of being fairly good perennials. However, they are generally considered short-term (annual) bedding plants, since they do not cope well with growing circumstances that are less than ideal.

Darwinhybrid

Single-flowered cultivars, long-stemmed, midseason flowering. Originally the result of hybridization between cultivars of the Darwin Group with *T. fosteriana* and the result of hybridization between other cultivars and botanical tulips, which have the same habit and in which the wild plant is not evident. We have to admit that this group of true perennials—the regal giants of the tulip kingdom—are our favorites. Among the largest and tallest tulips (18-24"), these midseason

The blackish-burgundy petals of Triumph T. 'Gavota' are trimmed with sulphur yellow but occasionally vary with pink or white shadings on the edges—quite a color!

bloomers make a most impressive show in the landscape, and we find that during a long, cool spring in Virginia, our Darwinhybrids stay in bloom for four or five weeks. We have seen many instances around the country—with the exception of the warmest zones, 9 and 10—where these tulips have perennialized and bloomed faithfully for 15 to 20 years under good growing conditions *(see section on Culture)*. Some companies have dubbed them "perennial tulips." Darwinhybrid tulips produce new bulblets before they bloom, hence the little bulbs develop better and perennialize well. They also tend to be virus- and disease-resistant.

Single Late
Single-flowered cultivars, mainly long-stemmed, late flowering. This group includes the Darwin Groups and Cottage Groups of the past. It also includes the popular Scheeper's hybrids (French tulips), many of which are *tetraploid* (bigger and more vigorous) with extra-long stems. Their late blooming offers a large choice of companion plants in the garden.

Lily-Flowering
Single-flowered cultivars, midseason or late flowering, flowers with pointed reflexed tepals. Stem of variable length. Almond-shaped blossoms with pointed and tapered petaloids date back to 1799. These lovely, graceful flowers are perfect for gardens and flower arrangements.

Fringed
Single-flowered cultivars, tepals are edged with crystal-shaped fringes, midseason or late flowering. Stem of variable length. Because of the fringes on the edges of the tulip's petals, this group is quite eye-catching. Some multi-flowering cultivars are included in this group.

Viridiflora
Single-flowered cultivars with partly greenish tepals. Late flowering. Stem of variable length. These flowers are increasingly in demand. Their subtle colors are perfect for gardeners who prefer an understated palette. The blending of green throughout makes them easy to use with many other plants and flowering trees.

The color medley of cherry red, plum purple, and rich cream give this luscious Lily-Flowering T. 'Yonina' great appeal.

Rembrandt

Cultivars with broken flowers, striped or marked brown, bronze, black, red, pink or purple on red, white or yellow ground, caused by virus infection. Long-stemmed. Rembrandts are not commercially available and are seen only in historical collections. A great deal of time has been given to hybridizing efforts to create new, healthy cultivars that have a similar look as the old Rembrandt types that took the world by storm.

Parrot

Single-flowered cultivars with laciniate, curled, and twisted tepals. Mainly late flowering. Stem of variable length. Originally known as "parakeet" tulips, they date back to 1672. We find that bloom time can span from early-midseason to late blooming. With the exception of *T.* 'Estella Rijnveld,' most are "sports" (chance mutations) from Single Early and Triumph or Single Late types.

Double Late

Double-flowered cultivars. Late flowering. Mainly long-stemmed. Some mid-season and shorter stemmed cultivars now fall into this category. These long-lasting, peony-type blossoms make marvelous cut flowers and bedding plants.

Kaufmanniana

Tulipa kaufmanniana *with her cultivars, subspecies, varieties, and hybrids, which resemble* T. kaufmanniana. *Very early flowering, sometimes with mottled foliage. Flower with multicolored base opens fully. Exterior normally with a clear carmine blush. Height up to 20cm.* Generally, the flowers of this type bloom very close to ground level and are superb for bedding or forcing and for pot or container culture.

Fosteriana

Tulipa fosteriana *with her cultivars, subspecies, varieties, and hybrids, which resemble* T. fosteriana. *Early flowering, leaves very broad, green or grey-green, sometimes mottled or striped. Stem medium to long. Large, long flower, base variable. Fosteriana* are good perennializers and make great cut flowers. They are happy in the garden as a bedding plant with other early blooming companions.

T. 'Black Parrot' is a multi-purpose tulip. It creates an illusion of shade in a sunny garden, it's wonderful for elegant flower arrangements, and it shows up beautifully in the spring garden, especially when planted in front of lighter-colored flowers.

Greigii

Tulipa greigii *with her cultivars, subspecies, varieties, and hybrids, which resemble* T. greigii. *Mostly with mottled or striped foliage, flowering later than* Kaufmanniana. *Leaves spreading normally on the ground, mostly strongly undulated. Flower shape variable.* Many plants are purchased for their foliage only and this is one group whose foliage is attractive before, during and after bloom, which makes it more valuable for a longer period of time in the garden. These tulips bloom from early midseason to midseason with a few late cultivars thrown in. They make superb bedding and container plants, with most types forcing fairly well.

Miscellaneous

In fact not a cultivar group, but the collection of all species, varieties, and their cultivars, in which the wild species is evident, not belonging to any of the above-mentioned cultivar groups. Most species tulips tend to perennialize and naturalize better than some of the hybrids when planted in climates and soils similar to those where they grew in the wild. These are the tulips for berms, rock gardens, the fronts of borders, and container gardens.

Other Tulips

Multi-flowered

Although there is no separate division that groups multi-flowered tulips, there are some that naturally produce more than one flower per stem. Some types of tulips will produce multiple flowers when their bulbs are very large, although their show isn't consistent. If bulbs are given a heat treatment, they will sometimes produce multiple flowers as well. Some of the multi-flowered tulips we adore are:

T. *bifolia,* T. 'Candy Club,' T. 'Colour Spectacle,' T. 'Georgette,' T. *hageri* 'Splendens,' T. 'Happy Family,' T. *humilis* 'Liliput,' T. 'Modern Style,' T. *orphanidea* 'Flava,' T. *polychroma,* T. *praestans* 'Fusilier,' T. 'Merry-Go-Round,' T. 'Orange Bouquet,' T. *praestans* 'Unicum,' T. 'Red Bouquet,' T. *tarda,* T. 'Titty's Star,' T. 'Toronto,' T. *turkestanica,* T. *urumiensis,* T. 'Wallflower,' T. 'Weisse Berliner.'

One of the reasons that T. clusiana *var.* chrysantha *is one of our favorites is because the sunny yellow, bright interior is so inviting during the day. We also enjoy the soft crimson exterior petals when the flower closes in the late afternoon —almost like having two flowers in one!*

Miniatures and heirlooms

Most species tulips qualify as miniatures as most flowers are under 1½" across and are usually under 8" tall. These smaller flowers have numerous and variable uses in the garden and are as colorful and as eye-catching as their larger relatives when planted *en masse*. Some of our favorites are:

T. albertii, T. altaica, T. bakeri 'Lilac Wonder,' *T. batalinii* (various sorts), *T. clusiana* (various sorts), *T. humilis* (various sorts), *T. kolpakowskiana, T. linifolia, T. maximowiczii, T. praestans* (various sorts), *T. tarda, T. turkestanica* and *T. wilsoniana*. There are several new varieties that are a bit larger, but are certainly not as large as the standards. *T.* 'Lady Jane,' *T.* 'Little Beauty,' *T.* 'Little Princess,' *T.* 'Tinka' and *T.* 'Titty's Star' are the new kids on the block that are causing quite a stir because of their visual impact in the garden and their ease in adapting to various garden conditions.

Bulb Sizes

Bulb size is usually directly connected to the size and quality of the bloom that will emerge from it. Tulip bulbs are priced and sold in sizes determined by measuring the bulb's circumference in centimeters. Large-sized bulbs like the Darwinhybrids and the Giant Single Late cultivars produce large flowers, with the expected bulb size of 12/14cm. or 14/16cm. Larger bulbs sometimes produce multi-flowered stems in certain cultivars. And, if they are a lot larger, they often produce an extra leaf that can alter the look of the blossom. Conversely, if the bulb is smaller than standard size, the flower is also generally smaller and the bulb produces fewer flowers per stem.

Cultivars that have smaller flowers such as Kaufmannianas, Greigiis and species normally produce smaller (10/12cm.) bulbs. Be sure your source reveals the bulb sizes so you will know what to expect.

Tulip bulbs grown in clay soil often

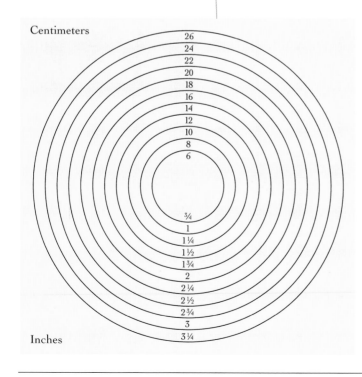

Centimeters

26
24
22
20
18
16
14
12
10
8
6

¾
1
1¼
1½
1¾
2
2¼
2½
2¾
3
3¼

Inches

produce bulbs with unattractive skins, but we understand they often perform better in the garden and for forcing. It's difficult to import clay-grown bulbs to the U.S. because clay soil is difficult to clean from bulbs, and the USDA will not allow any soil on imported bulbs and plants. Growers in The Netherlands have tried planting tulip bulbs in netting, but, even with this aid, they are difficult to clean. Tulips grown in sand produce prettier bulbs that are easy to clean and are therefore the bulbs sent to the U.S. and Canada for the most part.

Gourmet Tulips

Tulip bulbs are edible, which is why gardeners have a difficult time staying ahead of voles, rabbits, and deer and keeping bulbs in their gardens. In fact, tulip bulbs sustained some Dutch families and became a staple for others during the German occupation of The Netherlands during World War II. Tulip petals, along with other edible flowers such as nasturtiums and chive blossoms, make a nice addition to salads according to our friend Cathy Barash, who writes about edible gardening. With endless colors from which to choose, and a slightly different flavor for each type of tulip, salad can become a work of art as well as a culinary delight! At a recent garden party, we made an hors d'oeuvre of orange tulip petals topped with salmon spread for our guests to enjoy. We've also found that tulips with fragrance seem to have the best taste. So be sure to smell and taste-test before you serve your guests a colorful surprise. (Please note: If you plan to include exotic, colorful tulip petals in your next salad, be sure you are an organic gardener and aren't using systemic pesticides.)

Our daughter, Dorothy, tastes T. 'Generaal de Wet.'

Fragrant Tulips

Most tulips have a moderate fragrance that is pleasantly reminiscent of green and growing things. Some tulips, however, have an incredibly sweet, musky, or fruity fragrance that can perfume a room. It's no wonder that fragrant tulips and other flowers are so popular. We find that flowers of all types, including tulips, are more fragrant on warm days, although the flowers last longer if the weather is cool. If the day is cool, you may have to breathe some warmth on the flower before inhaling to help it release its fragrance. You may want to try: Peach Blossom, Monte Carlo, Generaal de Wet or Prinses Irene.

III. *Tulip Culture*

When to Plant

Unfortunately, the Christmas season seems to get started a little earlier every year as merchants attempt to capture the first sales of the season. Likewise, many believe that the garden center displaying the first bulbs wins more sales. This happens sometimes as early as Labor Day, when it's still 90°F or higher in many areas of the country and the ground temperature is too hot to plant. However, if your favorite tulip is displayed and you don't buy it, it might be sold out later. So, what do you do? Perhaps your merchant will agree to let you buy the bulbs and store them for you until the ground temperature cools. If you take them home, be sure to keep them dry, in a cool, 50-70°F well-ventilated area. If you have any doubts, put a fan on them: there's no such thing as too much ventilation. By keeping them dry, you will help eliminate the danger of the tulip bulbs contracting a fungus-related disease *(see section on Diseases)*.

Planting time in the fall varies according to climate *(see Cultural Recommendations by Region)*. Generally speaking, planting should not occur until the soil temperature in your area is 60°F or less at 6-12" deep. This is usually after the first heavy frost, but three to four weeks before the soil freezes solid. A bulb may be stressed if planted in soil that is too warm and damp at the same time. On the other hand, bulbs need to form roots before the ground freezes. Once roots are initiated, the bulb's cellular walls join, becoming more elastic and resistant to freezing. This is one of those wonders of nature that most of us do not understand but still think is a marvel and give thanks for. In cold zones 2 and 3 bulbs can go in earlier, but as a general rule, they are best planted in zones 4—7 from October to November with warm zones 8 and 9 waiting until December or January. It may feel a bit colder than you like, but your bulbs will be happy.

If consumers push suppliers to get tulips out earlier each year,

Opposite: Fosteriana T. 'Orange Emperor' with its oblong, sturdy, tawny brushed orange flowers, is a great perennial tulip in our gardens and combines well with daffodils as well as T. 'Don Quichotte' and other bright-colored tulips.

A beautiful driveway garden is a real spirit lifter for anyone coming home at the end of a hard day.

then suppliers will push growers to dig them earlier and earlier. Eventually, the tulip crop will suffer. Tulip bulbs need a certain amount of time to finish their development before being dug in the summer. Importantly, tulip bulbs need time for the bloom to initiate and develop within the bulb after digging and before planting. The very best quality bulbs may not be available in August, but should be ready by September and October.

Where to Plant

Design

Many tulips, with their tough, upright stems and perfectly formed flowers lend themselves nicely to formal planting and geometric designs. You can become a garden artist using your trowel as your brush, your tulip bulbs as your palette, and your garden as your canvas. The possibilities are endless! Wherever you decide to plant, keep these general hints in mind: Plant at least ten tulips in a group. Space bulbs three times their width apart (approx. 3") in a garden or border that will be viewed from 10 to 20 feet away. If a landscape planting will be viewed from 50 to 100 feet or more away, you will need 50-100 or more bulbs planted in one group for a good visual effect. Do not be tempted to take your bag of 10 bulbs and make them "stretch" by planting them too far apart. The result will be a weak, disappointing presentation. Instead, pick a small site that is highly visible to develop one year, then select and develop another site the following year.

Most individual tulip flowers last between two and four weeks. Their duration is largely dependent on the temperature during bloom time. Flowers also tend to last longer when nighttime temperatures remain low. Naturally, if any specific day is very hot, dry, and windy, the flower's petals will lose moisture and bloom time will decrease. In general, the more substance (thickness of petals and sepals) the flower has, the longer it lasts.

Think about the following areas when trying to decide where to plant your combination tulip garden.
- The bank near your driveway or sidewalk. You will see your garden frequently and your friends and neighbors will, too.
- A lamppost garden near your entranceway

"Welcome Garden," smiles at the neighbors.

- A mailbox garden is one that you'll visit at least six days a week.
- A front door garden is a happy, friendly welcome to all who enter your home.
- A garden viewed from a kitchen window will be frequently seen.
- An island garden in your lawn will provide a break in your sea of green.
- A raised patio planter or a portable garden can be placed and enjoyed almost anywhere *(see section on Containers)*.
- A window box is a living flower arrangement *(see section on Containers)*.
- A street-side garden to greet you, friends, and neighbors is a place to share smiles and a happy contribution to your community.

Containers

Outdoor containers Little is brighter or more cheerful in the months of March, April, and May than the presence of containers chock-full of beautiful tulips around the patio, along your walkways, on either side of the entrance to your home or your driveway, or as accent points in your garden. Many tulips lend themselves well to container gardening if proper precautions are taken and a few simple rules of culture are followed.

- Select short-stemmed or low-growing cultivars that will have less of a tendency to fall or blow over. Our favored groups include Single Early, Double Early, some Triumphs, Kaufmanniana, Greigii, and most species.
- Select a container with enough soil volume to protect bulbs from great temperature fluctuations in the winter. If the container is large enough, even large-type tulips will have enough room to grow properly.

Large, stationary containers, or ones that are permanent fixtures above ground-level.

- *Insulation* Add a layer of foam insulation to the inside perimeter of the container before adding soil. This provides a thermal break that will help keep the container uniformly cool during premature seasonal temperature variation. Also, a layer of white pebbles, marble chips, or other reflective material placed on the soil surface after planting will help maintain uniform temperature and keep

Opposite: Elevated retaining wall garden

your flowers clean.

- *Size* A 6" pot normally holds five bulbs nicely; an 8" pot holds about 11 bulbs. The larger the container, the more bulbs should be used, in order to produce the best show. You can often plant them in the container in which they will be displayed, or they can be pre-grown in smaller, individual pots and later added to a large container if you live in an area where winters are severe or unstable.

- *Soil mix and water* It's best to use a sterile potting mixture that is coarse enough to drain well. Containers will need to be watered regularly; the smaller the container, the more often it will need to be watered. It's possible to extend the time between watering with the use of gels and granular, diatomaceous earth designed to release water when the soil becomes dry. Wicking is a self-watering mechanism in which one end of the wick is placed in the pot and the other in a container of water. If you're away or don't have time to water, this may be a solution for you.

- *Mulching* helps prevent weeds and holds moisture. The use of marble chips may keep the container from getting too hot by reflecting the sun's rays instead of absorbing them.

- *Fertilization* is important to plants of all types. Plants perform best when given proper, regular nutrition—just as people do. Slow-release fertilizer is best. Or, you can use a liquid fertilizer every couple of weeks when watering your container.

A lovely, full pot of T. *'West Point' and* N. *'Petrel' overwintered in a cooler at North Carolina Arboretum*

Moveable containers (overwintered in a mulch pile or a uniformly cool garage or polystyrene cooler)

- *Window boxes* Using multiple window box liners enables you to have a sequence of bloom all during the flowering season.

- *Pots and planters* Use liner pots to fit your decorative pots or baskets.

- *Individual pots* Cell packs 2" x 2" x 3" deep are good for starting your bulbs, especially for the gardener who enjoys combining different types of bulbs to create living flower arrangements (*see section on Pre-treating Bulbs at Home*).

- *Soil* Use coarse, well-draining growing medium with bark/peat/sand/perlite and/or vermiculite with the addition of a ceramic moisture enhancer.

- *Planting* Whether you use small, individual pots or 10" bulb pans, place the bulb on top of the soil so the roots can utilize all the soil.

- *Cover* with a layer of gravel or marble chips—the weight may keep the pots from overturning during windy weather.
- *Water* well at least once. Cover with a thick (6-12") layer of mulch or leaves, or place in a consistently cool area such as a garage for winterization.
- *As spring approaches,* gradually pull the mulch away to expose the emerging leaves to sunlight. Remove the pots from the mulch or garage and place them around your home as they are, or place them in decorative containers.

Places to use containers outside

Balconies

Windowsills

Patios

Porches

Poolside

An old wheelbarrow makes an attractive planter.

Walkways

Gardens

Doorways and entrances

Steps and stairways

Nestled in tree roots

Rock gardens

Woodland plantings

Community gardens

Places to use containers inside

Dining room table

End tables

Sunporches

Sickroom

Soils and Soil Amendments

Tulips perform best in alkaline to neutral sites. If you do not know your soil's pH, you may want to contact your county agent for information on getting it tested. Tulips also prefer good, fertile, well-drained, sandy loam with plenty of humus (well decomposed organic matter), especially at the root level. Unfortunately, few of us have the ideal soil situation. Do not despair! You can amend most situations—with the exception of extremely wet soils—to be perfectly suitable for good tulip culture. Where soils are poorly drained or where heavy clay persists, deep planting would be both difficult and stressful for the bulbs. In this case, one solution is to improve the top layer of the soil, plant the bulbs in the shallower, improved soil, and berm up over them (cover with additional soil or sand, creating a raised bed). This can both create a properly drained site and give the bulbs sufficient depth. When thinking about your soil and whether or not to amend it, remember that tulips need to be dry during the summer months when they're dormant. If they are in soil that retains a lot of moisture from summer thunderstorms or regular irrigation, the bulbs will likely become stressed or contract a fungus disease that may cause them to rot (*see section on Diseases*).

Organic Soil Amendments

Heavy clay soils should be amended with lots of organic matter (compost, composted bio-solids, fine pine bark, leaf mold), in addition to good topsoil or sand. These layers of several inches of organic matter and sand should be incorporated (tilled or spaded) into the clay to create a good blend of all amendments and the original clay. It's also helpful to add a layer of decomposed leaves or other fully decomposed material to the area each year, gently working it into the top layer. We ask soil to give something to us each year—we need to remember to give something back! If we feed our soil, it can supply the nutrients that, along with air, ample moisture, and sunlight, tulip bulbs need to manufacture their food.

How to Plant Your Tulips

Handle a tulip bulb like an egg or a delicate piece of fruit. They can bruise from rough handling, which makes them susceptible to developing a fungus that can damage and rot the bulb *(see section on Diseases)*.

Depth and Proximity

Brent plants bulbs in a radial design in Becky's "Teaching Garden."

Over the years the rule of thumb, "three times the height of the bulb deep and three times the width of the bulb apart," has been established as the proper depth for bulbs. This rule generally holds true except for some tulips whose bulbs benefit from a deeper planting of "four times the height deep" in good soil. The pressure increases as you dig down, so bulbs planted deeper (at least 8-12" to the bottom) often bloom for many more years because the bulbs tend to split up less readily. The bulbs also receive protection from rodents who normally work the top 3-4" of soil and seldom burrow 8-12" in search of edibles. And, with extra insulating soil, bulbs are buffered from the stress of severe climates and therefore less subject to disease. Deep planting's other advantage is that it allows sufficient space to layer—overplant and interplant—the tulips with companion bulbs, perennials, annuals, and ground covers. These will help mask the maturing tulip foliage, absorb extra rainwater to keep the tulip bulbs dry during dormancy, and provide shade during the hot summer months. (An important note: Tulip roots are non-contractile, which means they can't pull themselves to the proper depth. We must do it for them at planting. If you have difficulty digging deeply enough, provide extra depth by adding more soil or mulch on top.)

Proper Tools

Many types of tools are available for planting tulip bulbs. The hand-held, tubular type is designed only to plant very small quantities, and if you plant more than a few or in heavy soils, it will probably break or raise blisters on your hands. Inexpensive planters are meant to last for a couple of years, but the best are meant to last for a lifetime. If you have a few bulbs and are only planting once, the hand-held, inexpensive, thin steel type found at local garden centers is adequate. Most cone-shaped tools, whether hand-held or foot-powered, light-weight or heavy-duty, are designed to be used in soil that has been well-prepared or tilled and is relatively free from roots or rocks. If you are one of the lucky ones with near-perfect soil, sometimes after a rain you can dig planting holes without preparing the soil by using a heavy-duty tubular planter. We recommend choosing one with a stainless steel cone that is a bit larger at the top than at the bottom and about 10-12" long. This will allow the dirt to flow through easier. Also, be sure that it has nothing over the top of the cone that may impair the soil from flowing through. Look for one that has a foot bar on either side of the cone, handles with good grips, and a very sturdy body. The easiest way to use this tool is to place it on the ground in the spot where you want to grow a bulb, step on the foot bar to push it down into the ground, twist and pull up. At this point, you should have a cone full of dirt. *(Don't turn it upside-down to dump out the dirt—this is a wasted step.)* Place the cone on the ground and repeat the process, digging the next hole. The dirt already in the cone should flow out the top, fall on the ground, and then be used to refill the previous hole in which a bulb has been placed.

Spade-like implements, or what we call "naturalizing tools," can be used in unprepared soils, around the base of trees, and in ground covers. If you should hit a rock or root while using this tool, it's easy

Becky layers bulbs in deep holes made with a heavy-duty bulb planter.

to just turn it at a slightly different angle to cut the hole for the bulb. Choose one that has a 10-12" narrow blade with pointed, sharp cutting edges made from a strong material. Those with foot bars on either side of the cutting surface and handles with good grips are easier to use and more efficient. The appropriate method of use for these tools is placement on top of the ground at a 90° angle where the bulb is to be planted. Next, step on the foot bar and push the blade into the ground. Pull the handles back toward you to a 45° angle (you'll see a bit of soil lift up at the end of the blade). Then, with your foot on the bar, force the blade the rest of the way into the ground and shove the handles away from you, pushing the hump of soil aside, creating a V- or U-shaped hole that is about 10" deep—perfect for tulips.

A 2"x 8" stainless steel trowel is another favorite tool for tulip planting. Hold the trowel like a dagger, stab it into well-worked soil, pull the trowel handle toward you and put the bulb into the hole that's created behind the "blade."

Water

There are two important times when it will be absolutely necessary to water your tulips, in order for the bulbs to produce beautiful flowers in forthcoming seasons. The first is right after planting in the fall, when the root system needs significant moisture to begin to form in preparation for the winter chill. Usually one good, soaking rain or watering is sufficient to get the rooting process started. The second opportunity is in the spring, when the plant begins to sprout and push through the earth, and continues until the foliage begins to turn yellow. Tulip bulbs need about $\frac{1}{2}$" of rain or water per week for optimum growth. If they receive less, the plants will not reach their maximum height, and the flowers will not achieve their full potential. If you're watering, we recommend the use of a leaky pipe or soaker hose as this gets the water to the roots where it is needed and not on the leaves. Too much water on the leaves and flowers during warm spring days and nights can make the tulip more susceptible to botrytis, a very damaging leaf fungus *(see section on Diseases)*. The need for water ends in the summer months when bulbs are dormant and prefer to be completely dry. In an area that receives significant rainfall during the summer, it's best to put lots of other plants in the same

ensure a continuous supply of nutrients that will keep your tulips performing optimally.

Weeding

While weeds growing in your garden may be unsightly, you need not worry about them hurting your bulbs unless the weeds rob the tulip of vital nutrients or water or grow in an invasive, choking, or light-blocking manner. Chickweed, nettle, vetch, and rye grass are ones that we have to watch for in our zone. Some say that any plant growing where it's not wanted is a weed. Hen-bit, field cress, and wild Johnny-jump-ups, although classified as weeds, produce pretty flowers that we think complement or add shoes, socks, and pants to the sometimes naked-looking tulip plant. Since they're not choking or invasive, we just leave them and enjoy the addition of their flowers. Once they pass their prime in early summer, they're easy to remove by huge handfuls, or what we call "gross weeding"—the opposite of fine weeding.

Because we live right on a saltwater tributary of the Chesapeake Bay, we don't use any chemicals, with the exception of occasional spot use for persistent perennial weeds. We have developed the garden design philosophy, "If you put enough plant material in the garden, there is less room for weeds." Many people ask us about what pre-emergent herbicides are appropriate to use with tulips, and some are registered for use with flower bulbs. Climatic and soil conditions and laws pertaining to herbicides vary so much throughout the U.S. that we recommend you check with a USDA agent in your area. A pesticide license may be required to buy and apply certain chemicals recommended for tulip bulbs. Careful companion planting, use of mulch, and a bit of judicious weeding at the right time is our preference for an environmentally friendly, beautiful, and fun garden.

Deadheading Blooms and Maturing Foliage

Insects are frequent visitors to tulip flowers for their nectar. In the process of gathering nectar, the tulips are hybridized or pollinated, and subsequently seeds are formed. If you want your flowers to be beautiful year after year, it is very important to snap off the fading blooms and immature seed pods. Otherwise, over one-third of the bulb's energy will be channeled into making seed rather than back

into the bulb, in the form of starches and sugars, to provide for next year's bloom. It is equally important to let the leaves remain intact until maturity when the foliage begins to turn yellow and flop over. At this time, they have finished photosynthesis and may be safely removed without depriving the bulb of nutrients. This process usually takes eight to ten weeks after flowering, depending on climatic conditions. Also, for disease prevention, it's important to remove falling flowers and flopping foliage from your garden *(see section on Diseases)*.

Digging Bulbs

One does not need to dig and divide tulips on an annual basis, as some garden books advise. However, if you must dig bulbs either to keep them from rotting during a wet summer, to move them to another location, or to rearrange them for appearance, transplanting is best done as the foliage turns yellow but before it completely disappears.

Holding the foliage with one hand, insert a digging fork or spade *(see section on Tools)* into the soil about 4-6" away from the bulb and dig straight down at least 8-10" deep. Pull back on the handle of the tool to pry the bulb and surrounding soil loose, so that the bulb will slip out without breaking away from the stem and leaves. Treat bulbs tenderly to avoid damage and gently shake off any remaining dirt. If you aren't going to regularly irrigate their new home, you may replant the same day. If you decide to wait until fall, place the bulbs loosely in mesh bags or on screen-wire trays out of direct sunlight (to protect the bulbs from sunburn), in a dry area with plenty of air circulation. We prefer to use a fan to dry them quickly. Keep them in a dry area where the air doesn't get stale because air movement in storage is very important. The presence of a fan helps to remove gases from the bulbs' normal respiration, which is important for their health.

Do not cool or refrigerate at this stage because bulbs still need warmth to aid development of their future buds. Keep the bulbs away from ripening fruit or decaying vegetation that may give off ethylene gas and cause the bulbs to abort next spring's bloom.

Replanting Tulip Bulbs

In the fall, planting instructions are similar for tulip bulbs that have just been dug and those that have been stored all summer. First, shake or gently rub off any remaining dirt. If the bulbs are physically

attached, bulb to bulb, don't force them to separate. Like parent and child, they will separate when the time is right. However, do gently untangle intertwined roots. Plant them 6-10" deep, depending on their size. Small, young bulbs the size of nickels or dimes should be placed at a shallower depth until they mature, but those the size of quarters and fifty-cent pieces should go the full depth. *(See section on Planting.)*

Pests

Both tulip bulbs and flowers are edible, which means hungry animals in your area may be drawn to your garden for a midnight snack. My Dad often reminded us of the likelihood of animals eating some of what we planted, since their ancestors inhabited our garden long before we did. His suggestion, whether it be tulip bulbs, corn or beans, was to plant enough for yourself and then add a few more for the critters! That's an inclusive and companionable thought, but if God's creatures are taking more than their share from your garden, read on!

Voles

When tulips disappear, moles are often blamed. However, moles eat only grubs and worms in your lawn or garden. The real "underground bulb monster" is a little mouse-like critter, the vole. There

Levi, our vole catcher, anxiously watches a vole hole.

are two types of voles: the meadow vole *(microtus pennsylvanicus)*, which looks like a field mouse with a long tail and large ears, and the pine vole *(microtus pinetorum)*, which has a short body, a blunt head, and very small ears. These little animals are prolific (a gestation period of about 16 days), seem to be omnivorous, are seldom seen (primarily subterranean), and voracious!

There is a good chance voles are in your garden if some—or all—of your favorite plants disappear. Vole presence is confirmed by 1" diameter holes in the ground. (As a child, I used to think they were snake holes!) Moles may push up the soil and produce raised ridges in your lawn as they tunnel for insect larvae, grubs, and worms; but voles are the culprits for decimating plant material.

Voles seem to come and go in cycles, but once you have them, getting rid of them is not easy. We have been testing several products designed to deter them, but at this point the jury is still out! Spray-on or liquid products applied to the bulbs before planting assured a lovely, colorful display the first spring. The following year, our bloom was disappointing, since there was evidence that the protective solution had washed away with the yearly rain and the voles had returned to feast. Fortunately, not every bulb was eaten. We still had some spring color, thanks to the surviving tulips.

Voles have tender pads on the bottoms of their little feet, and they apparently don't like to dig through sharp gravel. A relatively new product made of tiny, sharp pieces of expanded slate is supposed to deter voles from digging to get to the desired plant. We have used it in beds without a lot of success. However, we have also used it as a top layer for potted tulips, and this seems to keep both the voles and mice at bay.

If you think that you may have voles, think twice before you mulch your tulips. It can be an invitation to a warm winter haven with tulips and other edible plants as the winter feast. You may want to wait until late winter or early spring to mulch those beds.

Deer

Deer are an increasing problem all over the country. We have taken away their fields and forests and have built houses, shopping centers, and super highways. At the same time that we've eliminated their natural predators, population density has made hunting unsafe. Deer

have adapted by learning to search for food in neighborhoods instead of at forest edges. Deer fencing at the edge of the woods helps keep them out of the garden. One type of fencing now on the market is virtually invisible from a distance and not an eyesore. Crumpled chicken wire placed on the ground around the perimeter of the property is often a deterrent, because deer don't like to get their hoofs caught in it. We have also seen yellow electric ribbon fencing for horses surrounding a nursery. During the winter, when there are no plants to eat, the electric fence is baited with peanut butter. The deer are attracted to the peanut butter, but the shock scares them off. Later, when the plants and trees begin showing tender, tasty shoots, the electric fencing is turned off, but remains enough of a reminder to stop the deer from bothering the plants. Perhaps this fencing isn't the best solution, but it works without chemicals and without real harm! If there is an alternate source of food, it seems that deer can be trained.

Bad-tasting sprays help keep deer and rabbits from eating tulip flowers. However, these must be reapplied after a rain. It is also more effective to switch repellants every few weeks, as critters seem to adapt to them after a period of time. Natural repellants like composted sewage sludge (bio-solids), soap, garlic, red pepper, human hair, and predator urine may all help for a short time. Ultimately, we will need to do a better job of managing the deer herds that are reportedly greater in number now than when the first settlers reached our shores.

Disease

Commercially grown tulip bulbs are dug in the summer, usually in July, and quickly dried with a forced-air system. Then they are cleaned, graded, counted, packaged, and transported in refrigerated containers to the United States and Canada. After the containers arrive, they are unloaded and sorted so each specific order can be shipped. During this process, as the bulbs go through various temperatures and conditions, they will sometimes develop a blue/gray mold on their surfaces. If the mold can be wiped off, it is usually not detrimental to the bulb or its development.

You may encounter the fungal disease botrytis—known as "tulip fire" or "the common cold of tulips,"—if your garden bulbs have

Tulips with spotted and distorted leaves—signs of botrytis

been stressed by a poor environment or damaged by mishandling. Most tulips carry the spores, just as we carry common cold germs, which is why stress is enough to induce development of the disease. Botrytis manifests itself first by necrotic lesions, which are irregular, round circles of discoloration on the bulbs under the tunic. Bulbs with these lesions should be sorted out and discarded to protect the rest of the batch from infection. The first sign of a fungus attack is spotting, shriveling, yellowing, or browning on the tips of the leaves shortly after they emerge and then grayish spots on the leaves as they open. (Note that brown tips on the foliage, with no further symptoms, may be caused by sudden freezing temperatures.) The opening flowers will appear spotted, and eventually the whole plant will become covered with fungus, shrivel up, and die. In the meantime, spores may spread to tulip plants nearby and into the soil. As soon as you see signs of disease, it is best to pick off the leaves and destroy them, dig up the bulb and destroy it, or spray with appropriate fungicides. Check with your local county agricultural service for recommendation of the fungicides registered for use in your area.

When the tulip flowers naturally fade and begin to die, pick them off and remove them from the garden. If the flower petals fall off on the ground and begin to decompose around the base of the tulip plant, they could cause next year's tulips to contract botrytis.

Prevention is usually the best cure, and the following precautions will help to keep your tulips free from botrytis.

Virused Rembrandt tulip next to a healthy one

- Purchase your bulbs from a reputable supplier.
- Be sure they are in good health—firm and unblemished.
- If you can't plant right away, keep bulbs cool (50-70°F) and dry. Avoid storage near fruits and vegetables as the ripening process gives off ethylene gases that may cause the tulips to abort their blooms.
- Be sure there is good air circulation, and, if in doubt, put a fan on the bulbs.
- Plant after soil temperature reaches 60°F or less at 6" deep.
- Plant deeply in well-drained soil, rich in decomposed organic matter.
- Place where the tulips will get good air circulation while in leaf and flower.
- Keep pests and other animals away from the plants. Bruised leaves are very susceptible to fungal attack.
- Do not replant sections where there were diseased bulbs for at

least five years as spores may remain in the soil and infect new plantings. If you absolutely must plant the same area, use a soil fungicide to drench the ground and a systemic fungicide dip to soak the new bulbs prior to placement.

- Try not to put tulips in the same area every year so spores of botrytis will not build up in the soil. This is the same idea as crop rotation employed by farmers.
- Remove all spent tulip flowers as they can spread botrytis when they decompose.
- Remove all tulip leaves when they begin to turn yellow and flop over. Rotting leaves may allow botrytis spores to collect at the base of the stem.
- Avoid overhead irrigation, which can encourage fungal disease problems.
- Select tulip cultivars rated less susceptible to fungal problems.

Fusarium

Another tulip sickness encountered when bulbs have been stressed is *Fusarium oxysporum tulipae,* or bulb rot. This fungus seems to be ever present, so when opportunity presents itself, the spores germinate and attack the bulb. They consume the sugary tissues of the bulb, reducing it to a dried-out, dead shell that often crumbles to a powder. Bulbs are most likely to contract the fungus when they have been bruised or stressed in handling or shipment.

Outward signs of the disease are white necrotic lesions on the bulbs and a sweet smell emanating from stored bulbs. The disease first becomes apparent in sunken brown lesions (wounds) on the outermost fleshy scales of the bulb. The lesions grow until they reach the basal plate, or bottom, of the bulbs, and from there spread throughout. Infected and rotting bulbs give off ethylene gas that can cause nearby bulbs to abort their future blooms. Remove infected bulbs from the rest and destroy them.

IV. *Cultural Recommendations by Region*

Northeastern United States and Eastern Canada

Congratulations! You live in an area perfect for tulips! With cold winters, often long, cool springs, and adequate rainfall, tulips have a close to perfect environment in which to perform and often perennialize.

Keep in mind the following tips when selecting your tulip garden site. Choose a site that is in full, or almost full, sun and be sure the soil is well-drained. Plant in the fall anytime after temperatures at night cool down to 40-50°F but about four to six weeks prior to the ground freezing. This should give the bulbs ample time to begin the rooting process, which will keep them from freezing during the severe winter weather. Apply a slow-release fertilizer to the top of the bed after planting. We recommend Holland Bulb Booster® or Brent and Becky's Bulb Supplement *(see section on Fertilizers)* and water to help rooting get started.

After the ground cools but before it freezes, cover your beds with a lightweight mulch such as pine needles, chopped leaves, or buckwheat hulls to help keep the soil temperature uniformly cool all winter. Mulch also helps to retain moisture in the soil and cuts down on weeds. However, if your tulip bulbs seem to disappear and you suspect underground visitors are enjoying their taste, you may want to forgo mulch as it may be the critters' invitation to stay for the winter *(see section on Pests)*.

Almost any tulip can perform well in these zones. You have endless possibilities for color combinations, bloom times, heights, shapes,

The colorful beauty and wonderful fragrance of the many types of tulips displayed at The New York Botanical Garden, Bronx, NY, thrill this visitor.

Opposite: Bright, shimmering red Triumph T. 'Dynamite' is enhanced by the presence of the smaller, softer-colored T. clusiana var. chrysantha 'Tubergen's Gem'.

Brookside Gardens, Wheaton, MD, in the mid-Atlantic area, displays perennial tulips.

and sizes, so be creative and plant some Monet or Rembrandt garden art in your landscape.

Mid-Atlantic

This is a very good climate for tulips, with cold winters and moderate springs that meet most tulips' requirements for chilling and photosynthesis, ensuring that they will perform well. Because summer thunderstorms and downpours are typical, we suggest that tulips be interplanted or combined with drought-tolerant annuals or summer blooming bulbs and perennials that will take advantage of summer rainstorms but do not require daily watering. For optimal, repeat performance, tulips need to be dry during dormancy. Companion plants will soak up summer moisture and provide shade during the hottest part of the year.

Most types of tulips will perform nicely in this area. However, we find the best are the Darwinhybrid, Single and Double Early, tetraploid Single Late, Kaufmanniana, Fosteriana, and many species types.

Southeast

This section of the country typically has hot, moist summers and cool, moderate winters. If the appropriate cultivars are chosen, tulips can be perennial in certain areas. There are some cultivars that don't require an extremely long cold period to trigger their blooms, while others don't mind the long, hot summers. However, it is a must for tulips to be dry during their dormancy *(see section on Culture)*. If you have an automatic irrigation system, be sure to place your tulips away from its reach. Also, succulents and other plants that do not require daily watering interspersed with the tulips will help absorb moisture from summer storms.

Early blooming cultivars, Darwinhybrids and tetraploid Single Late types perform the most reliably in this area.

"Snow-birds" adore tulips, which are almost impossible to grow in Florida. Cypress Gardens in Florida solved this problem by devising a "fun-filled fantasy tulip garden."

North-Central United States and Canada

Here, cold winter temperatures trigger bloom in all types of tulips without any problem, but they will sometimes suffer from strong

winds and extreme climatic changes in early spring. Choosing short, sturdy tulips is appropriate to these conditions. Also, while late bloomers can eliminate the problems that come with spring freezes, their blossoms may not last as long if a spring heat wave hits.

Chicago Botanic Garden has glorious gardens filled with tulips like T. 'Blushing Lady' and T. 'Maureen' for visitors to enjoy.

Midcentral and Great Plains

Adequate rainfall, long, cool winters and hot summers are characteristic of this region, which also has some of the richest soil in the United States. Tulips of all types should perform well in these conditions, provided they are planted in time to root sufficiently before the ground freezes hard. Plant your tulip bulbs when the ground temperature has cooled to 60°F or lower for best results—late September through mid-October are about the appropriate time. Afterward, water well so the tulips will begin initiating roots right away *(see section on Culture)*.

South-Central

The south-central and Gulf Coast regions can be problematic when trying to plan gardens using tulips as perennials. The somewhat alkaline soil often present in this region is suitable for tulips and we have been told by many who live in the area that *T. saxitilis* is one species tulip that is persistent. However, winters here are frequently not cold enough to trigger the tulip's blooming mechanism. So, in order to have luscious, colorful tulips in the spring, they may have to be treated as annuals and chilled for eight to 12 weeks before planting *(see section on Forcing)*. Some companies offer pre-cooled bulbs for planting late in the season and, when you consider the value of your time, this may be a cost-effective option. It is important to plant the pre-cooled tulip bulbs just as soon as possible, because once taken out of the cold they begin to lose the cooling effect and may even begin to grow.

When making your cultivar selection, keep in mind that the earlier blooming the tulip, generally the cooler the weather and the longer lasting the flowers. Of course you can extend the season by choosing early, midseason, and late bloomers.

Central-Pacific, Pacific Northwest, and Western Canada

In coastal northern California, Oregon, Washington, and Canada long, cool, wet winters and springs followed by relatively moderate, dry summers and falls, create an almost ideal tulip climate. In this region, there are fairly large tulip production fields in the Puyallup and Skagit Valleys.

If you live in an area with heavy clay soil, we strongly suggest that you not only amend it, but also raise the level of the planting areas to

Gardeners in the South Central U.S. have reported success with tulips such as T. bakeri 'Lilac Wonder.'

ensure good drainage. Plant bulbs in the fall when temperatures at night stay between 40-50°F or when the soil temperature at 6-8" is between 40 and 60°F. Begin while the weather is still nice, but before the rainy season, when planting bulbs may not be as pleasant. If the soil is dry when you are planting, water the beds to make sure the tulips take root. Covering your beds with a light mulch of ground leaves, evergreen needles, or other light, plant-based material will keep down the weeds and help the soil temperature remain consistent.

Arid West and Southwest

This area encompasses Eastern Washington, Eastern Oregon, Eastern California, Western Idaho, Nevada, Western New Mexico, Arizona, and Western Colorado. Relatively long, cool winters, very hot to moderately hot, dry summers, and low moisture present challenges for growing tulips. The addition of drip irrigation in the spring while the tulips are actively growing should help create a much happier environment. Your dry summer is very good for the dormancy requirement of tulip bulbs. Be sure to water in the fall after planting to help the bulbs establish roots.

Naturalized and Perennialized Tulips

We use the term "naturalize" to mean increase by underground division or by re-seeding and spreading naturally aboveground. We use the term "perennialize" to mean bloom year after year and increase only by division. If you live in an area where tulips seem to live forever, where there are no problems with voles or deer and where long, chilly springs with cool nights are typical, species tulips are the appropriate choice for naturalization. They will find your area comfortable and will re-seed, and make an ever-blooming, colorful colony. Don't deadhead these tulips, but allow their seed to disperse and spread. Of course, other types of tulips will also perennialize under favorable conditions, and if pollinated by wind or insects, will produce hybrids that will spread and continue the spring show.

In spite of the voles that adore our sandy loam, we have managed to keep some tulips blooming for years. Our most successful have been the Darwinhybrid, Single Early, Double Early, Fosteriana, Kaufmanniana, species, and Greigii tulips.

In the southwest area of the U.S., T. clusiana chrysantha 'Tubergen's Gem' is reported to perennialize.

Darwinhybrids, which come in many colors, are often the most reliably perennial for us.

v. *In the Company of Tulips*

Companion Plantings

The tulip flower is of great beauty, but, standing alone in a garden, it is reminiscent of a solitary soldier standing guard. Tulips need to be interspersed with companion plants to achieve the best visual effect. But how do you choose which plants and other bulbs to bloom along with your tulips?

It's possible to achieve a succession of tulip bloom for 14 to 16 weeks by carefully selecting the very earliest species and combining them in a garden with early, midseason, late, and very late cultivars. Once you find a group of plants that have similar cultural requirements, the critical issues become color, height, and bloom time. Color, although slightly variable according to the site, can be more constant than height, which is influenced by the richness of the soil, its moisture, exposure, and available nutrients. Bloom time can be altered by the time of planting, weather, and of course, cultivar choice.

If your spring starts in late February and lasts until late May, that's almost three months to have early, midseason, and late flowers and will make it more difficult to achieve the simultaneous blooming of different flowers. If you normally have a long winter, a short, four- or five-week spring and an early summer, then getting flowers to bloom together will be less of a challenge. With these points in mind, here are some lists and hints for bulbs, perennials, and other companions to bloom with your tulips, as well as suggestions to extend the blooming season.

An entire chorus of tulips, daffodils and other spring-flowering bulbs makes quite a concert of color.

Opposite: The contrasting colors of late-blooming Greigii T. *'Red Riding Hood,'* Narcissus (N.) *'Camelot,' and* Muscari latifolium *attract attention, embellish each other's features, and often strengthen the garden design.*

Pages 64-65: T. *'Come Back,' is a great perennial tulip and complements the flowers of other spring-flowering bulbs like* Fritillaria imperialis *'Lutea.'*

Differently shaped flowers with similar hues, such as Triumph T. 'Salmon Pearl' and T. 'Apricot Parrot,' create a serene garden.

Daffodils

Daffodils or *Narcissus*, (*N.*) are probably the most logical bulb choice to use as companions to tulips. Some say that having daffodils planted in the same garden as tulips may even help protect the tulip bulbs from voles! We're not sure that's always true, but they do complement each other's good looks! A few of our favorite combinations:

T. 'Hollandia' and *N.* 'Petrel'; T. 'Striped Bellona,' *N.* 'Quail' and *N.* 'Suzy'; T. 'Yellow Present' and *N.* 'Peaches and Cream'; T. 'Olympic Flame' and *N.* 'Tuesday's Child'; T. 'Toyota' and *N.* 'Intrigue' and T. 'Menton' and *N.* 'Queen of the North'

Combinations of tulips with similar blooming times

Many tulips are combined in a particular division because of their bloom time; i.e., Single Late Tulips and Double Early Tulips. Two tulips from the same division, especially the divisions that either have the term "early" or "late" in their name, will often bloom together. On the other hand, there are early, mid spring, and late blooming tulips labeled as Triumphs, so you must read catalogues and informational signs in garden centers carefully.

This is probably where we should repeat that there are no absolutes in the horticultural world, especially outdoors. We have experienced some springs when the weather has been so unusual that early tulips bloomed with late ones, just to prove that we were not in charge. A humbling experience, indeed! After experimenting, we're sure you'll find many of your own special combinations. In the meantime, here are a few we love:

T. 'Angelique' and T. 'Mount Tacoma'; T. 'Salmon Pearl' and T. 'Apricot Beauty'; T. 'Red Present' and T. 'Yellow Present'; T. 'Parade' and T. 'Golden Parade'; T. 'Temple of Beauty,' T. 'Blushing Lady,' T. 'Hocus Pocus' and T. 'Perestroyka'

Other bulbs to bloom with your tulips

Early—*Arum italicum*, Chionodoxa, Hyacinthus, early Daffodils, early Muscari,

Midseason—*Anemone blanda, Fritillaria imperialis,* Iris *bucharica,* Leucojum, midseason Daffodils, Ipheion, Fritillaria species, midseason Muscari,

Late—*Anemone coronaria,* Hyacinthoides, Camassia *cusickii,* early Allium, early Daffodils, late Muscari.

Other plants to provide a color echo
Combining a brilliant tulip with a plant of a similar color, echoing the hue of the tulip, doubles the garden's visual impact. Below are a few suggestions by color that will help make this type of design easier to envision and plan. Conversely, you can take the same list and build an area filled with color

A tiered garden with a very tall flower like T. 'Ballade' in the back, Lily-Flowering T. 'West Point' in the middle, and adorned with the shorter, beautiful blue Muscari armeniacum in the front prevents any one flower from blocking the other—and makes a splendid combination.

contrasts that will be equally effective. Remember, if you feel happy with the effect and the flowers look wonderful, then you've done a great job *(see Encyclopedia for tulip varieties).*

White: *Lunaria annua* 'Alba Variegata' ('Honesty' or 'Money Plant'), *Viola* x *Wittrockiana* (Pansy), *Viola cornuta* (Johnny Jump-up), *Bellis perennis* (English daisy), *Myosotis sylvatica* 'White Ball' (white 'Forget-me-not'), *Iberis sempervirens* (Candytuft), *Anemone sylvestris* (Snowdrop Windflower), *Arabis* (Rockcress), *Polygonatum* (Solomon's Seal), *Dicentra spectabilis* 'Alba' (White 'Bleeding Heart').

Blue/purple: *Brunnera macrophylla, Symphytum* (Comfrey), *Ajuga reptans* (Bugleweed), *Pulmonaria* (Lungwort, Jerusalem Sage), *Arabis* (Rockcress), *Vinca minor* 'Bowles Variety' (Periwinkle), *Vinca major* 'Jason Hill' (Periwinkle), *Aubretia, Viola cornuta* (Johnny Jump-up), *Primula* hybrids (Primrose, Cowslip), *Phlox divaricata* (Blue Phlox).

Red: *Dianthus barbatus* (Sweet William), *Aquilegia canadensis* (Columbine).

Pink: *Bergenia, Bellis perennis* (English Daisy), *Helleborus orientalis* (Lenten rose), *Dicentra* (Bleeding Heart), *Luneria annua* (Honesty or Money Plant).

Green: *Helleborus foetidus* (Bear's Claw), *Moluccella* (Bells of Ireland).

Yellow: *Primula* hybrids (Primrose, Cowslip), *Erysimum cheiri* (Wallflower), *Aurinia saxatilis* (Basket-of-Gold), *Doronicum*

(Leopard's Bane), *Trollius* (Globe Flower), *Euphorbia polychroma* (Cushion Spurge), *Ranunculus ficaria, Taraxacum* (Dandelion).

Flowering trees

Flowering trees and shrubs offer an exquisite backdrop to all of your flowers, especially those that bloom in spring. They will also make you feel as if you have a wealth of flower girls when their petals begin to decorate the ground.

Malus sylvestrus (Crab Apple), *Cornus* subsp. (Dogwood, various sorts), *Pyrus* subsp. (Pear), *Prunus* subsp. (Cherry), *Chaenomeles* (Flowering Quince), *Spiraea,* Wisteria, Magnolia.

Companion planting to extend the blooming season

It's possible to extend the color spectacle throughout the growing season with sun-loving bulbs, perennials, and annuals if you plant them in the fall right on top of where your tulips are planted. (Or, plant them in the pockets of soil around the tulip's ankles in the early spring; they will then grow to cover the area where the tulip is planted.) Don't worry, the tulips will come up right through ground-cover or around the perennial or smaller bulb. Keep in mind that you must not overwater this garden as tulips absolutely do not want to sit in hot, moist soil during their dormancy. Here are some of our favorite summer blooming plants:

Achimenes, Alstroemeria, Amarcrinum, Amaryllis Belladonna, Babiana, Bletilla, Canna, Chlidanthus, Coreopsis, Crinum, Crocosmia, Dahlia, Delphinium consolida (Larkspur), *Eucomis, Galtonia, Gladiolus, Habranthus, Hemerocallis, Hymenocallis, Incarvillea, Ixia,* Larkspur, *Lathyrus* (Sweet Pea), *Liatris,* Lily, *Lobelia erinus* (Edging Lobelia), *Lycoris,* Marigold, *Mathiola* (Stock), *Mirabilis, Nerine, Ornithogalum, Oxalis,* Petunia, *Phlox sublata* and *stolonifera* (Moss and creeping phlox), *Polianthes, Portulaca,* Rose, Queen Anne's Lace, *Scadoxus Sprekelia, Stachys byzantina* (Lamb's Ears), *Tigridia, Triteleia, Tritonia, Verbena, Zantedeschia,* and *Zephyranthes.*

The flowers of the rhododendron and Single Late T. *'Sauternes' match almost perfectly and together create quite a color spectacle.*

Opposite: The yellow color in Greigii T. *'Odia' echoes nicely with* Doronicum.

VI. *Forcing: How to Have Beautiful Blooms Out of Season*

Fooling the Flowers

Adventurous gardeners can have flowering tulips by carefully planning and forcing bulbs to have blooms by Christmas or even earlier.

Very early blooming is accomplished by using tulip bulbs that are suitable cultivars. These bulbs have been processed by the growers so that their cooling requirements have been met and they are ready to be potted indoors from November until February. You are only required to root them at cool temperatures (45°- 55°F) for two to three weeks until roots show at the bottom of the pot, and then put them in a sunny window. Mail order catalogues and garden centers will let you know by the descriptions and headings if this type of bulb is available. They will be called "pre-cooled" or "pre-treated" bulbs for forcing. If you find that you can't pot them right away, you must store them in a cool (40°F) place, or the bulbs will begin to lose their stored coolness and become regular tulip bulbs. In this case, the bulbs will either have to be planted outside for normal winter chill or the pre-cooling process will have to be started all over again. For the highest quality results, our best advice is to have the container and soil ready when the bulbs arrive, plus a good, cool area for rooting.

Pre-treating Bulbs at Home

In order for tulips to bloom indoors, they need to be pre-chilled or

Opposite: T. humilis *'Magenta Queen'* and many other small, species tulips like it, force easily when potted, buried in a deep mulch pile for about 12 weeks, and brought inside to add color to an otherwise dull winter day.

Pages 72-73: T. *'Peach Blossom,'* and T. *'Holland Ballet,'* look like cotton candy with their fluffy white and pink double flowers.

Greigii T. *'Plaisir' and* Muscari armeniacum *are naturally short, look great and behave nicely in pots.*

Providing every bulb with its own 2¹/₂" pot in which to pre-cool and generate a good root system throughout the winter, can result in lovely, long-lasting, living flower arrangements, patio planters, and window boxes.

given a cold period to fool them into thinking that they have been through normal winter weather. Many books have been written on the subject. Whether they were written for the professional in the business of forcing bulbs or the homeowner who only wants to force a few pots, experts usually agree that most tulips need approximately 12 to 16 weeks of cold (35°- 45°F) for best results.

There are several ways to force tulips successfully. Pot the bulbs in September, October or early November. (Follow the guideline of three bulbs per 4" pot; five bulbs per 6" pot; nine bulbs per 8" pot and 15 bulbs per 12" pot.) Fill the pots ⁷/₈ full of soil; place them on top of the soil, close together so their shoulders are touching. It is not necessary to cover the bulbs with soil, but it is important to have plenty of soil under the bulb for optimum root penetration. At this point, if there is a possibility of being visited by animals, you may want to spray the bulbs with repellent. Spread sand or gravel around the necks of the bulbs to help hold them in place and discourage disturbance by animals. Next, put the pots right on the ground outside in a shady area, water them well once, and cover them with 6-12" of pine straw, leaves or other light mulch. Leave for the required 12 to 16 weeks or until the bulbs have rooted, pull a little mulch away and bring a pot or two into the house and place in a sunny window. After those blooms are spent, bring in another group, and continue the process until spring.

A few words of caution: If you are in an area where the dreaded vole is a problem, be sure to protect your precious tulip bulbs from the critters by covering the pots with a piece of small-mesh wire before putting the mulch on top or spray the bulbs with bulb protector. Better still, do both! On another note, if spring begins to arrive before you have forced all the pots, pull the mulch away from the bulbs before they grow too much, otherwise they will have bleached, yellowish foliage like blanched asparagus. Exposure to sunlight is necessary for the foliage to have a luscious, rich green color.

Another way to utilize the same electricity-free, pre-cooling treatment is to plant each bulb in its own 2" pot, similar to an annual plug pot. This type of planting will enable you to use the bulbs in many more flexible ways. Fill each pot with a coarse potting mix (not a seedling mix) and put a tulip bulb on top of the soil. It is not necessary for the bulbs to be buried, only the roots need to be in the soil and will eventually fill the pot. Set the pots in nursery trays side by side to help them stay upright. Place the trays on the ground in a shady area on a groundcloth or landscape cloth, which may be helpful in keeping down weeds. Cover with gravel and vole block, if necessary. Water well once and cover with a thick layer of light mulch such as pine straw or leaves. Follow the instructions above for bringing them into the house.

A fiberglass container filled to the brim with T. *'Madame Lefeber' ('Red Emperor')*

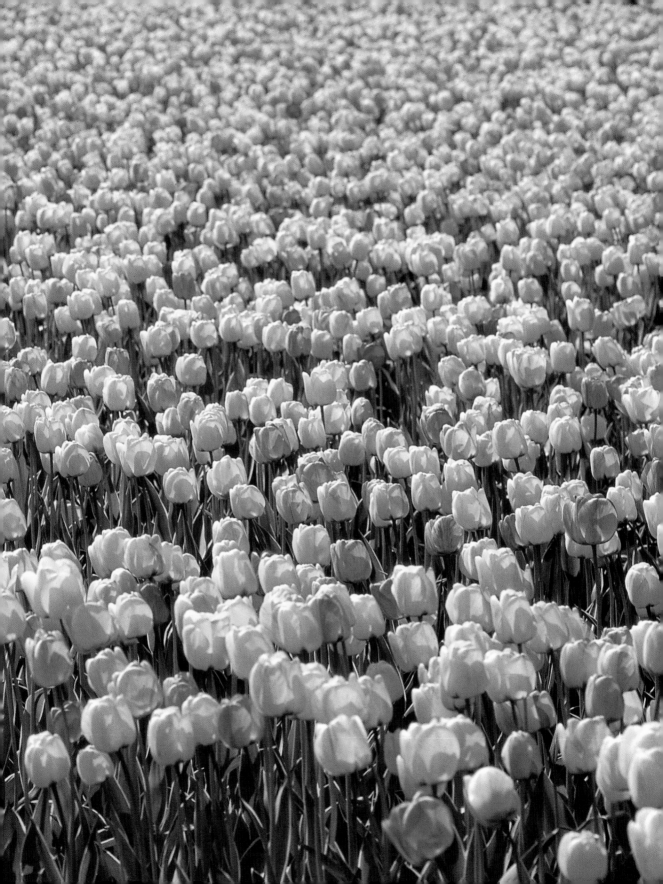

VII. *Hybridizing: Making New Tulips*

Although we ourselves are not actively involved in hybridizing tulips at the present, we thought it should still be part of the information in this book.

According to our sources, not much tulip hybridizing is going on in the United States. Most of the excitement about new hybrids comes from The Netherlands, where two groups in particular have been very generous in sharing their knowledge and enthusiasm. Arie Peterse, who is in charge of tulip hybridizing at the Hobaho's Testcentrum voor Siergewassen in Hillegomin, Holland, is making remarkable progress and has some really exciting cultivars that will be available in the future. Other groups, Vertuco and Remarkable, were formed by several large growers in Holland to combine their efforts, ideas and talents, and share the bulbs once a very special one is created and needs to be grown into larger stocks. New colors, color combinations, patterns, foliage, and fragrances are emerging in the trial crops of tulips. Other growers are also trying their hand at creating new tulips. We think the future is promising.

When creating a new tulip cultivar, it's helpful to have a goal in mind. Are you looking for a certain color combination? A particular bloom time, growth habit or height? Pick a day that is warm (65-75°F) and preferably not too windy to make your crosses. If the bees are flying, that's a good sign that conditions are right. For the best success rate, the flower should be freshly opened and not past its prime. The pistil should be slightly sticky so the pollen grains have an easier time taking hold. With your goal in mind, find flowers that

Opposite: Darwinhybrid T. 'Big Chief' has been a strong, repeat-blooming hybrid tulip in our garden.

Pages 78-79: T. 'Silverstream,' a Darwinhybrid tulip, is variable in color. This variation is enhanced by the contrast against its pinkish-white edged leaves —even in a seemingly endless field.

Arie Peterse gathers pollen from potential pollen parents for use in his efforts to produce future tulip hybrids.

have one or more of the characteristics you desire. Carefully remove the pollen from the flower that you are going to hybridize so it won't self-pollinate. Then, brush the pollen from the anther of the other tulip onto the sticky part of the pistil of the flower you are hybridizing. The pollen grains travel down the pistil in the tube leading to the ovary and the eggs are fertilized. Because tulips have nectar and pollen, they are eagerly visited by bees, so it is a good idea to wrap the fertilized flower with a gauze or foil covering to protect the desired cross from bees that may spread additional pollen and create a cross that you don't want. Next, write down the names of the parents so you won't forget, and mark the flower in which you put the pollen with a stake, garden label, or a flag to identify it easily.

Approximately six to eight weeks later, if your cross was successful, the seed pod should be fat, brown, and beginning to dry. Watch closely, because there is a fine line — just a few days — between harvesting too early or too late. If you harvest too early, the seeds may not be mature enough to germinate. If you harvest too late, the pods may pop open, spilling the seeds on the ground, where they are very difficult to find. When the pod has just a tiny opening, take action and gather the seeds immediately!

We find it more successful to plant the seeds right away in a light potting soil covered with about ¼" of sand and leave them in our cool greenhouse where it is easy to water and keep track of them. However, if you do not have a greenhouse, plant them outside in flats in a protected location and remember to water them. Seeds sown closely together seem to have a beneficial effect on each other and germinate better. After germinating, we leave them to grow close together for two to three years before separating them to plant outside and mature.

In the first year, each seed will produce only one leaf that resembles grass and one root that develops into a small bulblet. This tiny bulb, which will grow larger each year, usually takes five to seven years to mature to blooming size. Once a new hybrid shows promise for the markets of the future, it is propagated and multiplied by natural bulb division. On average, tulip bulbs double or triple annually in normal propagation. Micro propagation or tissue culture of tulip bulbs has not proven to be practical and, as we understand it, is not yet used in the bulb trade.

There are many hybridizers working with tulips in Holland, and their strong emphasis is on tulips for forcing because this is where the greatest demand and sales lie. Tulips most suitable for forcing are the naturally short and early cultivars, many of which fall into the Triumph classification—the reason why we are seeing more and more of this type. There is concern that in the future only Triumph tulips will be available for purchase. If we want to have an impact on future cultivars; i.e., make more Darwinhybrids available, then we'll have to increase our purchases now, in order to send a message to the growers and the hybridizers. While it is not romantic to think about, growing trends are definitely tied to economic issues. However, it does makes us consumers more powerful when we do act.

Arie Peterse uses a cotton swab to pollinate tulips at the Testcentrum in Lisse, The Netherlands.

A breeding house at the Testcentrum in Lisse, The Netherlands, where many hybridizing crosses take place every spring

VIII. *Flower Arranging and Festivals*

Cutting and Conditioning

Tulips are among the world's most popular cut flowers because of their bright, cheerful colors, reasonable price, and lasting quality. In order to enjoy your garden tulips inside and also have the bulbs perennialize, you must cut the flower stems above the leaves, leaving the leaves to mature and manufacture food for the next year's bloom. If you want longer stems and do not care about perennialization, simply grasp the tulip stem where it emerges from the ground and pull up firmly. The stem will normally break off near the bulb and give you about six extra inches of stem length with which to work. Most commercially grown tulips are actually pulled and not cut. Of course, if you choose a very tall tulip or mostly Single Late types to grow in your cutting garden, it's possible to cut the stalk above the leaves and still have a nice long stem for arranging purposes.

Once you have pulled or cut the stems or purchased tulip flowers, you should condition them before arranging in a vase. First, firmly wrap the stems of the flowers in a bunch with waxed or waterproof paper. Cut approximately ¼" off the bottom of the stems at a 45° angle to ensure the flower tubes are open and free to take up water and nutrients. Then, place in deep, tepid (slightly warm to the touch) water so the stems will harden off, stiffen, and stay straight in an arrangement. (The "old wives" trick of piercing the stem under the flower to keep the flower upright has proven to have no value.) If you are not concerned with the shape of the stem for your arrangement, you can condition the flowers without wrapping and

Opposite: Tulips have a strong impact at Lewis Ginter Botanical Garden in Richmond, VA.

Pages 84-85: Graceful Lily-flowered tulips, T. 'Mariette' and T. 'White Elegance,' bask behind a carpet of Anemone coronaria 'De Caen.'

Tulips of all colors, shapes, and sizes were pulled and arranged in a small bucket, then placed in a decorative basket. A warm welcome on any deck, porch, or front step.

the stems will generally retain the shape that takes hold in the water.

Vases and containers should always be kept clean, by using a solution of bleach or other disinfectant to eliminate bacteria that will clog the stem and hasten the flower's demise. The addition of a floral preservative to the water is helpful because it slows bacterial growth and generally has a nutrient that assists the flower's development. A couple of drops of bleach to one pint of water is another, less expensive way to cut down bacterial growth in the vase. One-half can of clear soda per one quart of water will also keep the flowers fresh. Carbolic acid, which gives soda its bubbles, prevents growth of bacteria, while sugar is a temporary nutrient.

Tulips should not be placed in water with fresh daffodils until the daffodil stems have hardened off and have stopped leaking the alkaloid sap that may shorten vase life. One to two hours in their own hardening-off bucket is usually sufficient to render daffodils safe to use with other flowers.

Even when tulip flowers are in vases, they tend to curve toward the light, so either select an evenly light spot to display your arrangement or turn it often to help retain the original positions. Also, tulips are heavy drinkers, so check the water level daily and add as necessary. Tulips that are picked in bud and showing color, continue to grow for a couple of days and should almost develop to their normal size.

Festivals

Starting a Spring Bulb Festival

In order to guarantee the success of a Spring Bulb Festival, it's a good idea to start planning well in advance. You might start by gathering together the top officers or other representatives of key organizations in your town to work up enthusiasm, develop a master plan, and divide responsibility for working out details of the various components. Suggested organizations include:

Mayor's Office

Chamber of Commerce

School Board

Parks and Recreation Department

All types of tulips are awesome in flower arrangements, but these Double Early tulips with hyacinths are exceptionally lovely and fragrant.

A street-side arrangement made with tulips in Oasis™

Garden Clubs

Other Civic Organizations

Developing Festival Ideas

Following are a few ideas to get you thinking about the kinds of festival events that would include everyone in your community, but we are sure you can come up with many more!

1. Schedule bulb plantings at schools. Every child can plant a bulb and take a bulb home to plant.
2. Select several dramatic sites in your community and fill them with enough bulbs to make a big splash of color. Possible sites are:

    banks alongside highways coming into town

    elevated median strips in town

    large planters arranged along a main thoroughfare in town
3. Schedule a contest for children to include

    flower arrangements

    artwork depicting tulips

Kingwood Center in Mansfield, OH, wows its visitors with lovely display gardens.

    a specimen exhibit of individual flowers

    pots of tulips

4. Organize a parade with children as participants decorating various items with tulip flowers:

    Dogs—"Magnificent Canines"

    Bicycles—"Beautiful Bike Floats"

    Lawnmowers—"Lovely Lawnmowers"

    Ponies and horses—"Prancing Steeds"

5. Get local merchants to donate prizes for the parade and flower shows.

6. Throw a 'Tulip Ball' and crown a 'Tulip Queen.'

7. Schedule a garden tour (Tiptoe Through the Tulips!) and sell tickets to visit the prettiest gardens in town.

8. Sell a collection of tulip bulbs as a fund-raiser.

9. Arrange a craft show requesting that each booth have some type of bulb flower theme.

10. Open a flower show to community participation. Each category can have separate men's, women's, and junior sections.

    arrangements

    specimen exhibits

    potted tulips competition

11. Sponsor lectures and workshops to teach and inspire potential gardeners in the art of having fun and success in the garden.

Putting the Proceeds to Good Use

Part of your profits could be used as working capital for next year's festival. The next logical choice would be to use some of the proceeds for community beautification. Bulbs, trees and other plants will not only beautify, but will also put more "oomph" in your welcome to all the visitors who come to your festival. When a community adds plantings and involves its residents in the project, an atmosphere is created that has a positive impact on the minds and moods of residents and visitors alike. Pride increases and litter is reduced, making it a "win-win" situation!

    Tulip festivals are usually held in midspring in the towns and cities listed below. We suggest you check websites, or local Chambers of Commerce, to find specific dates since they may change from year to year.

Holland, MI celebrates tulips at its annual Tulip Festival.

Michigan City, Indiana

Pella, Iowa

Orange City, Iowa

Holland, Michigan

Albany, New York

Pantego, North Carolina

Mount Vernon, Washington

Puyallup, Washington

Toronto, Canada

Spaulding, Lincolnshire, England

Hillegom, The Netherlands

If we have left out the festival that takes place in your hometown, we would really appreciate your letting us know so that we can include it in any future editions.

Tulip Gardens on Display

Over 500 cultivars and varieties of tulips are featured in our garden here in Gloucester, Virginia. There are also many botanical and public gardens that plant numerous tulip cultivars in attractive settings for their members and visitors to enjoy, as well as for educational purposes. A sampling of gardens where we have seen good tulip displays are:

Birmingham Botanical Garden, Birmingham, AL

Minter Gardens, British Columbia

Filoli Center, Woodside, CA

Denver Botanic Garden, Denver, CO

The Smithsonian Institution, Washington, DC

Atlanta Botanical Garden, Atlanta, GA

Callaway Gardens, Pine Mountain, GA

Chicago Botanic Garden, Glencoe, IL

Cantigny, Wheaton, IL

Des Moines Botanical Center, Des Moines, IA

Brookside Gardens, Wheaton, MD

Frederick Meijer Gardens, Grand Rapids, MI

Missouri Botanic Garden, St. Louis, MO

Biltmore Estate, Asheville, NC

The North Carolina Arboretum, Asheville, NC

Daniel Stowe Botanical Garden, Belmont, NC
Brooklyn Botanic Garden, Brooklyn, NY
Hofstra University Arboretum, Hempstead, NY
Conservatory Garden, Central Park, New York City, NY
Old Westbury Gardens, Old Westbury, NY
Kingwood Center, Mansfield, OH
Toledo Botanical Garden, Toledo, OH
Hershey Gardens, Hershey, PA
Longwood Gardens, Kennett Square, PA
Monticello, Charlottesville, VA
Norfolk Botanical Garden, Norfolk, VA
Agecroft Foundation, Richmond, VA
Lewis Ginter Botanical Garden, Richmond, VA
Maymont Foundation, Richmond, VA
Colonial Williamsburg, Williamsburg, VA
Boerner Botanical Garden, Hales Corners, WI

Longwood Gardens in Kennett Square, PA has a worldwide reputation for its inspirational garden displays, which include many types of tulips.

IX. *Recommended Tulips in Commercial Culture*

The cultivars recommended in this section, and in the book as a whole, were selected by using the following criteria:

1. We reviewed the cultivars grown in our own gardens and trials and chose the most successful.

2. We compiled customer recommendations and included their favorites.

3. We scanned mail order catalogues offering tulips and picked cultivars offered by at least four other companies.

4. We researched the Dutch growers list and presented tulips currently being grown by at least five growers.

We trust this reference will yield a list of garden-worthy tulips for North American gardens that will remain in commerce for a number of years to come. All photos were taken in gardens, in natural light. The color you see should be close to the color of the bloom in your garden. If you find one of your favorites absent from the list, there may be a similar one to fill that special spot in your garden and in your heart.

Opposite: In our opinion, mixtures of tulips are more attractive when the flowers bloom at the same time. In order to achieve this, plant bulbs of the same division, or those with similar bloom times. Here, T. 'Yellow Present' and its sport, T. 'Red Present'—which contrast vividly—put on a great show.

Division I:

Single Early

Overall Characteristics: These hardy, single-flowered cultivars bloom in early spring and many have a lovely, sweet fragrance. With mainly short stems, Single Early tulips are well-suited to pots, beds, and borders, as well as forcing indoors. Excellent Single Early cultivars:

'Bestseller' Muted tones of reddish/pink at the center, changing to rich orange, then to bright salmon. Sweet fragrance. Height 12"—14". Early midspring.

'Generaal de Wet' Musky, sweet fragrance. Soft marigold orange suffused with yellow. Heirloom 1904. Height 14"—16".

'Apricot Beauty' Soft salmon, fragrant with light rose flames on outer petals. Height 14"—16".

'Christmas Marvel' Super for forcing. Opens bright cherry, reddish/pink and matures with paler edge to petals. Height 12"—14".

'Mickey Mouse' Dark yellow tulip with distinctive blood-red flames. Rembrandt-type flowers that are smaller than others in this division. Height 10"—14".

'Beauty Queen' Rose feathered on pale salmon; fragrant sport of 'Apricot Beauty' but deeper in color. Height 14"—16".

'Flair' Large flowered, strong perennial. Vivid lobster-red on buttercup-yellow ground. Variable. Height 10"—12".

'Purple Prince' Deep bluish purple shade similar to grape juice. Petals have slight scalloping around edges. Height 12"—14".

Division II:

Double Early

Overall Characteristics: Hybrids of Single Early tulips, they share the short-stemmed characteristic and early-spring flowering habit. Flowers are usually semi-double to double and most are peony-shaped. Flowers measure 3-4" across when fully open. They present a colorful garden display and are exceptional for forcing. Excellent Double Early cultivars:

'Holland Ballet' Pure white with an occasional drop of 'butter' way down in the heart. Great for forcing and containers. Height 8"—12".

'Montreux' Soft primrose yellow. When mature, flowers may have a red glow. Height 14"—16".

'Abba' Glowing tomato-red with a yellow heart. Fragrant, multiple-petaled flower. Height 10"—12".

'Monsella' Canary yellow with blood-red flames and streaks in the middle of each petaloid. Sport of 'Monte Carlo.' Fragrant, one of the longest-lasting flowers in this division. Height 10"—12".

'Peach Blossom' Deep rose-pink suffused with creamy white and a yellow heart. Heirloom 1890. Height 8"—10".

'Holland Baby' Red/orange with a bit of yellow in the heart. A small tulip. Height 8"—10".

'Monte Carlo' Sulfur yellow. Multi-petaled flower with a terrific fragrance. World's most numerous tulip. Height 10"—12".

'Picasso' It's an incredible medley of soft, warm orange and apple-green leaves with a chartreuse edge. Height 8"—10".

'Yellow Baby' Rich buttery yellow. A real half-pint—about half the size of the popular 'Monte Carlo.' Height 8"—10".

Division III:

Triumph

Overall Characteristics: Single-flowered cultivars with a sturdy stem of medium height, Triumph tulips flower in mid-season. The most widely grown and hybridized group of tulips today, they have a wide range of colors and long-lasting flowers. Excellent for forcing and seasonal bedding color. Most are considered annual plants since they do not cope well with less than ideal growing conditions. Excellent Triumph cultivars:

'Annie Schilder' Rich, deep burnt orange with an edge of soft salmon. Superbly fragrant. Height 14"—16".

'Arabian Mystery' Rich, deep concord-grape purple edged with a shroud of white like a sheik in headdress. Height 14"—16".

'Attila' Moderate purple/violet when grown outside; a bit darker when forced. Large, showy flower with a dark stem. Height 16"—18".

'Barcelona' Bright fuchsia with a primrose-yellow base. A very strong tulip. Height 18"—20".

'Bastogne' Deep, rich blood-red with a yellow base. Classic tulip shape. Sturdy, with light fragrance. Height 12"—14".

'Bellona' Golden yellow flowers with sweet fragrance. Long-lasting, excellent cut flowers, good for forcing. Height 16"—18". Heirloom 1944.

'Blue Ribbon' Rich, deep purplish pink. A true "Blue Ribbon" winner for its strong constitution and excellent form. Height. 12"—14".

'Calgary' Pure snow white. Very short with large flowers. Great for forcing and pot culture. Height 8"—10".

'Couleur Cardinal' Deep scarlet with a plum blush, a dark base and stem. Fragrant and long-lasting. Heirloom 1845. Height 12"—13".

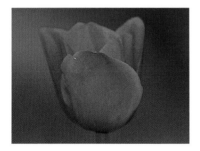

'Don Quichotte' Dark, dusky rose with hint of a purple hue. Tall and strong. Height 18"—20".

'Dreaming Maid' Violet petals with white edges. Height 18"—20".

'Dynamite' Shimmering red set off by a small, ivory base. Height 16"—18".

'Francoise' Large, long, egg-shaped, creamy white flower with a flame of soft sulfur yellow. Height 18"—24".

'Gavota' Long, deep plum burgundy with a white-edged yellow band on the petals. From Czechoslovakia. Fusarium-resistant. Height 16"—18".

'Golden Melody' Rich buttercup-yellow flowers like sunshine in spring. Height 14"—16".

'Happy Family' Purplish pink and dusky rose, sometimes with a fine white line. Multi-flowering with one large flower (the "daddy"), one medium flower (the "mom"), and several small flowers ("the children"). Easy to force. Height 14"—16".

'Hollandia' Shining blood-red with a yellow base and purple anthers. Height 14"—16".

'Jan Reus' Rich, deep red with a mist-like blush. Very dark reddish-black stem. Height 14"—16".

'Leen van der Mark' Rich, dark blood-red, frosted white on the edges and inside of its petals. An excellent forcer. Height 14"—16".

'Ile de France' Bright cardinal-red on the outside and darker blood-red on the inside. Easy to force. Height 14"—16". Early midspring.

'Jimmy' A colorful blend of carmine, rose, jasper, and orange with a lemon-yellow base. Height 12"—14".

'Mary Belle' Strong deep red tulip with a cheddar cheese orange-yellow edge. Excellent forcer and showy garden flower. Height 14"—16".

'Inzell' Ivory white, sometimes with a bit of violet blush at the base and a tiny violet line. Excellent and favorite forcer. Height 15"—16".

'Kees Nelis' Deep blood-red with a broad edge of glowing, golden-orange. Superb for forcing, cut flowers. Popular for over 50 years. Height 14"—16".

'Merry-Go-Round' Showy blood-red with a buttercup heart. One of the best multi-flowering tulips with as many as 5-8 blossoms per stem. Great for forcing. Height 14"—16".

'Nairobi' Bold, dark lipstick-red with a darker red stem. Height 14"—16".

'Passionale' Lilac purple with a tiny creamy white base. Height 14"—16".

'Red Bouquet' Bright signal-red with a small yellow base. A multi-flowered beauty. Height 16"—18".

'Negrita' Reddish purple in the garden, darker purple when forced. Height 14"—16".

'Peer Gynt' Reddish purple melting to soft, silvery edges. Dark, sturdy stems and a long-lasting flower. Height 16"—18".

'Red Present' Deep, rich cardinal-red with a yellow base. Shown here with 'Yellow Present,' the flower from which it is a sport. Height 14"—16".

'New Design' Pink with pale, creamy yellow base. Darker pink inside. Special white-tinged-pink edges to the leaves. Attractive foliage plant, like a hosta, before, during, and after bloom. Height 14"—16".

'Prinses Irene' Bright orange with purple flames, a sport of 'Couleur Cardinal.' Fragrant, Rembrandt type. Height 12"—14".

'Rosalie' Soft phlox-pink petals on a lighter rose ground with a creamy base. Height 14"—16".

'Salmon Pearl' Carmine-rose outer petals edged with coral. Inside nasturtium gold. Great forcer with lovely fragrance. Height 12"—14".

'Sevilla' Large, bowl-shaped flower opens deep rose, later changes to rich, dark-reddish color with pinkish blush. Height 14"—16".

'Shirley' Ivory white with small purple edge and blush. Variable, Rembrandt type, sometimes looking mostly white and other times with lavender streaks and flecks. Height 16"—18".

'Striped Bellona' Rich, buttercup yellow suffused with flames of bright blood-red. Striking Rembrandt-type tulip with a sweet, musky fragrance. Height 14"—18".

'The Mounties' Raspberry red with an ivory base. Height 16"—18".

'Washington' Elongated, egg-shaped flower of bold gold with opulent flames of blood red. Height 14"—16".

'Yellow Cab' Medium yellow, the color of taxis found in large cities across the U.S. Height 14"—18".

'Yellow Present' Creamy yellow with a luminous yellow interior. A very strong grower. Height 12"—14."

'Yokohama' Bright, Indian yellow with pointy petals. Strong flower with sturdy stems. Height 12"—14".

Division IV:

Darwinhybrid

Overall Characteristics: The most popular garden tulip. Midspring blooming flowers are deep, egg-shaped cups on tall, sturdy stems. Noted for their wide range of brilliantly colored flowers, larger than those of other divisions. Outstanding as cut flowers, they are widely cultivated for this use. Among the most perennial of all garden tulips. Excellent Darwinhybrid cultivars:

'Ad Rem' Large, round, showy flower. Brilliant orange/scarlet petals edged in shimmering gold. Fragrant. Height 20"—24".

'Apeldoorn' Vivid cherry to signal-red. Yellow-edged black heart. Old, popular favorite. Height 18"—20".

'Apeldoorn's Elite' Bright red with brilliant gold trim and a yellow-edged black heart. Sport of 'Apeldoorn.' Height 18"—20".

'Banja Luka' Rich blood-red flames on golden-bronze petals. Excellent perennial. Height 15"—17". Early-midspring bloomer.

'Beauty of Apeldoorn' Variable tulip—sometimes solid yellow, often touched with scarlet streaks; sometimes solid red. Height 18"—20".

'Big Chief' Frosty, rosy salmon with silver blush and a creamy yellow base. Variable color depending on the season. Height 20"—22".

'Burning Heart' Creamy with large red flames. Interior yellow with red flames. Rembrandt type. Vigorous grower. Height 18"—20".

'Come-Back' Blood-red with a tiny greenish-yellow base. Named because it does come back reliably. Height 16"—18".

'Daydream' Sunny yellow on opening, gradually maturing to soft apricot. Mildly fragrant. Height 18"—20".

'Golden Oxford' Pure golden yellow with occasional tiny red edge or flush. Inside yellow with black anthers. Height 18"—20".

'Holland's Glorie' Very dark red flower with a reddish-orange edge, yellow outer base. A virtual giant in this group. Height 18"—22".

'Garant' Bright golden/canary yellow flowers. Fern-green leaves with bold golden edge, creating its own color echo. Height 16"—18".

'Golden Parade' Pale buttercup yellow. Inside yellow with a black heart and anthers. Height 20"—22".

'Ivory Floradale' Opens creamy yellow and matures to ivory white. Large, classic form. Height 20"—22".

'Golden Apeldoorn' Primrose yellow exterior. Golden yellow inside. Black heart and an occasional red flush. Great for mass plantings. Height 12"—24".

'Gudoshnik' Chameleon-like flowers of red, yellow, yellow-streaked and spotted-red. Looks like a mixture blooming all at once. Height 20"—24".

'Ollioules' Old-fashioned rose with silvery white edges. Very large and elegant. Midseason bloomer. Height 18"—20".

'Olympic Flame' Mimosa yellow with signal-red flames. Variable, Rembrandt type. Height 18"—20".

'Orange Sun' Pure orange, the color of a summer sunset. Sunny yellow on the inside. Wonderful fragrance. Height 16"—18".

'Oxford' Bright scarlet with a yellow base. Inside pepper red with yellow heart and black anthers. Height 18"—20".

'Parade' Signal-red with a yellow base. Inside red with yellow-edged, black heart. Height 20"—22".

'Pink Impression' Blend of several different shades of rose. Strong stems make it an excellent cut flower. Height 20"—24".

'Silverstream' Soft creamy yellow, sometimes streaked with red and white. Green leaves have pinkish white edges. Height 20"—22".

'World's Favourite' Tomato-red with a tiny pale yellow edge on the petals. Strong, straight stems. Height 16"—18".

Division V

Single Late

Overall Characteristics: This group of single-flowered cultivars is long-stemmed and late-flowering. Flowers come in a variety of shapes and almost any color known to tulips. There are also some unusual bicolored varieties. The Single Lates make great cut flowers. Excellent Single Late cultivars:

'Big Smile' Warm golden yellow, leaning toward an amber shade. A long, egg-shaped giant. Height 20"—22."

'Blushing Lady' Buff orange and yellow with a blushing rose flame. One of the tallest, lily-shaped. Height 30"—36."

'Candy Club' Crisp, clear ivory white with a greenish glow, often with a tiny line of pinkish purple on the edge of the petals. Multi-flowering. Height 16"—18".

'Colour Spectacle' Canary yellow with cardinal-red flames inside and out. Height 16"—20".

'Cum Laude' Dark campanula violet with a base of white and blue. Height 16"—18."

'Douglas Bader' Soft "baby girl" pink with even softer edges. Inside china rose with ivory base. Height 14"—16".

'Esther' Medium pink with lighter pink edges and a blue heart. A bit smaller than other tulips in this group. Height 14"—16."

'Georgette' Clear, medium yellow with variable red edges, brush marks, and spots. Multi-flowered. Height 16"—18."

'Kingsblood' Royal dark cherry with scarlet edges. Extra-long stems that are great for cutting. Height 20"—22".

'La Courtine' Radiant gold with a true Rembrandt-like flame of the richness of 'Kingsblood.' Elegant, large, egg-shaped flower. Height 22"—24."

'Maureen' Creamy white. Very long stemmed with large, oval-shaped flowers. Tetraploid, Height 25"—27".

'Perestroyka' Giant, lily-shaped flower the size of a hand. Rose-pink with shadings of peach and salmon. Lovely. Height 30"—36".

'Queen of Night' Deep velvety maroon with brownish hues. Not quite black but dark enough to add shadows to a sunny garden. Heirloom 1944. Height 20"—22".

'Menton' Varying shades of pink—from soft violet pink to old-fashioned rose and even shading to a slight salmon edge. Tetraploid. Height 24"—27".

'Picture' Lilac rose. Unusual, elegant, and gracefully shaped flower with almost scalloped petals. Height 15"—19".

'Renown' Reddish pink with paler edges. Very tall with long-lasting flowers. A vigorous grower. Height 25"—27".

'Mrs. John T. Scheepers' Luminous yellow. Perfectly formed. Tetraploid. Heirloom 1930. Height 22"—24".

'Pink Diamond' Rose purple with paler edges and a phlox-pink interior. Sport of 'Pink Supreme.' Height 18"—20".

'Sorbet' Rosy white flamed with cardinal-red. Rembrandt type. Height 22"—22".

'Temple of Beauty' Rich combination of shades of red and orange on a "Gulliver-sized," lily-shaped flower. Striking when planted near a brick wall. Height 30"—36".

'Temple's Favourite' Nasturtium-orange edge with a carmine-rose flame and a yellow base. A giant, lily-shaped flower. Height 23"—32".

'Toyota' Glowing combination of rose and red with a white edge. A very tall, hardy-growing beauty. Height 24"—36".

Division VI

Lily-Flowering

Overall Characteristics: Slender, almond-shaped blossoms with pointed, recurving petals characterize these single-flowered cultivars that bloom in mid or late spring. Their graceful flowers endear them to many gardeners and flower arrangers. This group does not have a large number of cultivars. Excellent Lily-flowered cultivars:

'Ballade' "Kool-Aid" purple, lily-shaped flower sporting a broad band of contrasting creamy white on its edge. Elegant. Height 14"—16".

'Ballerina' Rich blood-red with a salmon edge. Sweet fragrance. Height 14"—16".

'China Pink' Medium pink with a white heart. Height 16"—20".

'Elegant Lady' Butter-cream with a pale pink overlay. Graceful flower with slim, pointy petals. Height 16"—20".

'Fokker Fan Fan' Bright orange with blazing red flames and pointy petals. Fragrant. Height 16"—18".

'Mariette' Deep, satin rose with silvery white base and edges. Height 18"–20".

'Mona Lisa' Soft yellow, pointed petals with rich blood-red flames. Rembrandt-like. Height 14"–16".

'Queen of Sheba' Deepest oxblood-red, edged with glowing golden orange. Height 14"–18".

'Marilyn' White with reddish-purple flames and streaks. A Rembrandt type with pointy petals. Height 18"–20".

'Moonshine' Soft, creamy, porcelain yellow with a perfect starburst of rich lemon yellow on the inside. Height 14"–16".

'Red Shine' Glowing deep red set off by a tiny white base. A pointy-petaled tulip. Height 18"–20".

'Maytime' Reddish violet with narrow white edges and a small yellow base. Heirloom 1942. Height 18"–20".

'Pieter de Leur' Rich, deep satiny red. Early midspring. Height 12"–14".

'West Point' Primrose yellow. Very fragrant. Heirloom 1943. Height 18"–20".

'White Elegance' Sometimes opens with a creamy yellow flush but matures to ivory. Very elegant, especially when combined with other white flowers for an evening garden. Height 20"—22".

'Yonina' Combination of cherry red and plum purple with a rich cream edge. Height 14"—16".

Division VII

Fringed

Overall Characteristics: Petals edged with crystal-shaped fringes characterize these mainly single-flowered cultivars. The tulips in this group are mutants from various other groups so the stems are of variable length and flowering occurs midseason or late. There are some multi-flowering cultivars in this group. Excellent Fringed cultivars:

'Blue Heron' Soft violet with a lighter fringe. Deeper violet interior and a cobalt-blue edged white heart. Height 20"—22".

'Burgundy Lace' Rich wine-red. Long-lasting flowers, good perennial. Height 25"—27".

'Fancy Frills' Rose-pink with an ivory base. Height 16"—18".

'Fringed Elegance' Primrose yellow with an occasional red fleck or edge. A great perennial with Darwinhybrid genes. Height 20"—22".

'Maja' Rich cream with banana-yellow edges and fringes. Height 16"—18".

'Red Wing' Solid red. Looks like a male cardinal with his feathers a bit ruffled by the wind. Height 12"—14".

'Swan Wings' Pristine white with beautiful "lace" on the edges. A great forcer. Height 10"—14".

Division VIII

Viridiflora

Overall Characteristics: These unusual, single-flowered cultivars are distinguished by petals whose color includes some green. Their flowers, which bloom in late spring, last as long as three weeks, making them good cut flowers. Excellent Viridiflora cultivars:

'China Town' Soft rose-pink flamed in gray/green. Offset by leaves of pink and white variegation on a bold green leaf. Late midspring. Height 10"—12".

'Esperanto' Deep, old-rose red, contorted petals with flames of apple green and white on leaves of gray/green with a broad, creamy white edge. Unusual. Late midspring. Height 10"—12".

'Formosa' Rich yellow with a broad central shaft of lime green. A lily-shaped tulip. Height 12"—14".

'Groenland' (Greenland) Dusky rose enhanced with soft green flames. An excellent perennial. Height 18"—20".

'Spring Green' Ivory with apple-green feathered flames. Height 16"—18".

Division IX

Parrot

Overall Characteristics: Noted for their brilliant color, these single-flowered cultivars display serrated, toothed, or twisted petals. They are mainly late flowering with stems of variable length. The very large flowers are green as buds, opening to reveal vivid colors. The stems are fairly strong, but planting them in sheltered spots is recommended due to the flower size. Excellent Parrot cultivars:

'Blue Parrot' Blue violet with hints of lavender. Sport of 'Bleu Aimable.' Height 18"—20".

'Fantasy' Pastel combination of salmon to bubblegum-pink with feathers of apple-green and buff. Height 18"—20".

'Apricot Parrot' Rose, apricot, and yellow with medium green flecks and stripes. Height 16"—18".

'Carmine Parrot' Combination of carmine and cherry-red with a blue heart. Early flowering and very long lasting. Height 18"—20".

'Flaming Parrot' Primrose yellow, often maturing to creamy white, with crimson flames. Creamy yellow inside with blood-red flames. Strong stems. Height 25"—27".

'Black Parrot' Very dark burgundy with almost black flames and edges. Heirloom 1937. Height 18"—20".

'Estella Rijnveld' Broad, deep, Rembrandt-like flame on a creamy white, feathered flower. Stem often interestingly contorted. Right out of a classic Dutch Master's painting. Height 18"—20".

'Green Wave' Soft mauve pink with large, medium-green flames and a bit of white. Petals have scalloped edges. Height 16"—18".

'Weber's Parrot' Soft, creamy white with streaks and edges of soft to dark purplish pink. A mossy green base. Height 14"—16".

'White Parrot' Pure white with an occasional flush of apple-green. Petals have scalloped edges. Height 12"—14".

Division X
Double Late

General Characteristics: The cultivars of this group, known as peony-flowered tulips because of their shape, are usually large and always double. Mainly long-stemmed, they bloom late. Double late tulips do well in regions with cold winters and later springs. Planting in a sheltered spot protects the large flowers from wind and rain. Excellent Double Late cultivars:

'Allegretto' Dark oxblood-red with tarnished gold edges. A sturdy double tulip. Height 12"—14".

'Angelique' Pale, bluish pink with darker shades of pink, white, and sometimes creamy yellow interspersed. Variable color and fragrant. Perennializes in some climates. Height 14"—16".

'Black Hero' Large, glossy black petaloids with a few reddish black sepals. Fully double sport of 'Queen of Night.' Height 16"—20".

'Blue Diamond' Softball-size flower of violet-purple. Strong stem. Late midspring. Height 14"—18".

'Carnaval de Nice' The Rembrandt of double tulips. Rich, blood-red flames through full set of double, clear white petaloids. Large and strong. Late midspring. Height 16"—18".

'Creme Upstar' Pale yellow with cream and pale pink overlay and creamy yellow interior. Variable color and fragrant. All of the colors intensify as the flower matures. Height 12"—14".

'Lilac Perfection' Medium lilac-purple with a small white heart. Height 16"—18".

'Maywonder' Rose with a tiny white heart. A rose-shaped flower. Height 18"—20".

'Mount Tacoma' Ivory white with a creamy white heart. Height 14"—16".

'Orange Princess' Similar characteristics as *T.* 'Prinses Irene' including rich, nasturtium-orange flamed purplish red coloring and fragrance, except that this flower is doubled or even tripled. Height 12"—14".

'Red Princess' Deep, rich red with hints of black and a gray veil shrouding the outside petaloid. Fragrant, fully double sport of *T.* 'Couleur Cardinal.' Sturdy. Midspring. Height 12"—14".

'Uncle Tom' Dark maroon-red. Peony-like flower. Height 14"—15".

'Upstar' Pale pinkish purple and rose with an ivory base and edges. Height 14"—16".

'Wirosa' Dark wine-red with creamy edges. Height 10"—13".

Division XI:

Kaufmanniana

Overall Characteristics: These are excellent, colorful perennials that bloom with early and midspring daffodils. Generally very short with midsized blooms. Flowers are often star-shaped or waterlily-like. Kaufmannianas are great for rock gardens, pots, and window boxes. Excellent Kaufmanniana cultivars:

'Ancilla' Exterior is rose-red and soft pink; white inside with a distinctive yellow center encircled by a red ring. Resembles a water lily when fully open. Variable coloration. Height 6"—8".

'Fashion' Lovely, empire-rose tulip with purple veins and yellow base. Colorful addition to the garden. Height 8"—10".

'Heart's Delight' An eye-catcher with mottled foliage and a color combination of red, rose, and golden yellow. Height 6"—8".

'Johann Strauss' Blushing reddish pink and creamy white waterlily-like tulip with some mottling on the foliage. Early. Height 6"—8".

'Scarlet Baby' Blazing scarlet interior with sunny yellow heart; exterior has a flush of darker red. Height 6"—8".

'Showwinner' Bright, fire-engine red flower short in stature, big in looks. Perfect for pots. Height 6"—8". Early spring.

'Stresa' Outside flower petals deep golden yellow, sepals deep red. As it opens, inside color is golden yellow with a band of rich red in the heart. Height 6"—8". Early.

Division XII:

Fosteriana

Overall Characteristics: Early flowering, with very broad green or gray-green leaves, sometimes mottled or striped. Fosterianas have a large, long flower on a medium to long stem. They are among the best for forcing or perennializing in the early-midspring garden. Bloom time coincides with that of daffodils. Excellent Fosteriana cultivars:

'Easter Moon' Soft, warm yellow petals echo the creamy yellow edge on green leaves. Great perennializer. Early-midspring Height 11"–15".

'Flaming Purissima' Showy, long-lasting flower is rich cream streaked with narrow, raspberry streaks. Very variable; provides perfect color-coordinated mixture that blooms all at one time. Midspring. Height 14"–16".

'Juan' Bright, royal orange with a glowing yellow base; exceptionally beautiful purple, mottled foliage. A great show before, during, and after bloom. Height 14"–16".

'Madame Lefeber' ('Red Emperor'). Fiery red with tiny yellow-edged black heart. Great heirloom tulip for a patriotic garden. Heirloom 1931. Height 12"–14".

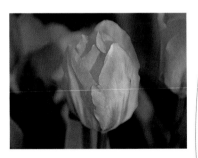

'Orange Emperor' Carrot-orange with buttercup-yellow base and flush. Height 12"–14".

'Purissima' ('White Emperor'). Lovely, pure white heirloom tulip with creamy yellow base and heart. We have seen clumps of this tulip 20 years old! Heirloom 1943. Height 14"–16".

'Solva' Color has been described as "orangish, pinkish red"! Unusual but beautiful, draws lots of attention; very long-lasting perennial. Height 14"–16".

'Sweetheart' Yummy combination of creamy white and creamy yellow. Height 12"–14".

'Yellow Purissima' Long, rich yellow flower with soft yellow flames. Perfect for pot or window box. Early midspring. Height 14"—16".

Division XIII:

Greigii

Overall Characteristics: Normally the strongly mottled or striped leaves spread on the ground, with variable flower shape. They have exceptional landscape value, even when not in bloom, thanks to their hosta-like leaves. Greigiis are one of the best tulips for bedding, patio containers, and in combination with midspring daffodils, anemones, and hyacinths. Excellent Greigii cultivars:

'Czaar Peter' Large, with claret/rose-red, pointed petals splashed and spotted with a creamy-to-clear white edging. Rosette of mottled, deep burgundy leaves. Striking, compact plant. Midspring. Height 8"—10".

'Zombie' Striped flower with red and yellow exterior and a buff rose interior with red-edged black heart. Strikingly beautiful and variable. Height 12"—14".

'Cape Cod' Yellow with buffy apricot hue and red flames; purple, mottled foliage. Height 10"—12".

'Donna Bella' Carmine-red sepals edged in creamy white with creamy petals tinged with yellow and a red-banded heart. Bold, dark, contrasting streaks in leaf cluster. Late midspring. Height 10"—12".

'Corsage' Soft coral, salmon, and apricot blend. Bold, burgundy-red markings pattern the rosette of attractive green leaves. Good window box choice. Midspring. Height 8"—10".

'Easter Surprise' Warm yellow petals intensify in color to tangerine at tips; enhanced with decorative, mottled leaves. Height 12"—14".

'Oratorio' Several shades of rose, almost watermelon, with deep purple, mottled leaves. Height 14"—16".

'Pinocchio' Bold, scarlet-flamed petals with white-edged, wavy sepals like a strawberry nestled in a bed of whipped cream. Softly mottled leaves. Midspring. Height 8"—10".

'Plaisir' Carmine red with sulfur edges often fading to ivory; black and yellow heart; colorful and variable. Height 8"—10".

'Red Riding Hood' Purple, mottled leaves; solid red flower with small black heart. Height 10"—12".

'Sweet Lady' Solid, compact, rectangular flower of pinkish/reddish/orange hue with a bright yellow base and center. Leaves uniformly mottled, reddish purple. Midspring. Height 6"—10".

'Toronto' Salmon-pink to ripe watermelon flowers; buttercup-yellow heart with bronzy green base; multi-flowered. Height 12"—14".

Division XIV:

Miscellaneous

Overall Characteristics: In fact not a cultivar group, but the collection of all tulips in which the wild species is evident, but not belonging to any of the cultivar groups. Generally excellent for rock gardens, the border front; forcing and containers. Many of these variable tulips are suitable for heirloom gardens. Excellent Miscellaneous cultivars:

albertii Orange/scarlet petals with yellow center. Heirloom 1877. Early flowering. Height 10"—12".

altaica Solid bronzy yellow interior; outer tepals often tinged carmine red; multi-flowered. Heirloom 1825. Midseason. Height 10"—12".

***bakeri* 'Lilac Wonder'** Sunny yellow heart and lilac-pink petals; great companion to daffodils 'Hawera,' 'Quail,' and silver-leafed plants like Stachys. Midseason. Height 6"—8".

***batalinii* 'Apricot Jewel'** Apricot/buff yellow petals with hint of rose; foliage in a rosette. Midseason. Height 4"—6".

***batalinii* 'Bright Gem'** Fragrant tulip with sulphur-yellow petals flushed with orange. Midspring. Height 4"—6".

***batalinii* 'Bronze Charm'** Little yellow tulip with bronzy feathering; wavy, gray leaves; fragrant. Midseason. Height 4"—6".

***batalinii* 'Red Gem'** Long-lasting, vermilion-red flower with a black base and blush on outside of petals. Late midspring. Height 4"—6".

biflora Early, tiny white with a yellow eye; similar coloring but smaller than *T. turkestanica;* multi-flowering. Heirloom 1776. Height 4"—6".

clusiana* var. *chrysantha Crimson exterior; bright yellow when open. Early-midspring. Height 6"—8". Heirloom 1948.

***clusiana* var. *chrysantha* 'Tubergen's Gem'** Exterior petals red, interior bright, sunny yellow. Larger clone of *T. chrysantha.* Midspring. Height 8"—10".

***clusiana* 'Cynthia'** Pinkish-red petals edged with chartreuse; purple base. Great grower and perennializer. Midspring. Height 8"—10".

hageri Multi-flowered, globe-shaped, coppery red flowers with greenish black centers over attractive rosette of rather glaucous, sometimes red-edged leaves. From the Eastern Mediterranean. Late mid-spring. Height 4"—6".

hageri 'Splendens' Coppery bronze, multi-flowered tulip with occasional green flames. Heirloom 1945. Midspring. Height 6"—8".

humilis Bright rose-pink with a yellow base; looks like a pink crocus. Plant with Crocus *vernus* and Iris *reticulata*. Heirloom 1844. Very early flowering. Height 4"—6".

humilis 'Alba Coerulea Oculata' Startling, small white flowers with a hint of steel blue and a dark, purplish black base. Slow to increase, but worth it. Midspring. Height 4"—6".

humilis 'Eastern Star' Magenta rose with a bronzy green flame on exterior and canary-yellow base. Early. Height 4"—6".

humilis 'Lilliput' Shining cardinal-red inside and out with a violet base. Early. Height 4"—6".

humilis 'Magenta Queen' Lilac purple with fern-green flame; lemon-yellow base. Early-mid season. Height 4"—6".

humilis 'Odalisque' Exterior red with a tin glow; interior beetroot purple with large, buttercup base and anthers; quite colorful. Citrus fragrance. Early midseason. Height 3"—4".

humilis 'Persian Pearl' A buttercup-yellow base supports magenta/rose petals; interior cyclamen purple; a colorful combination. Midspring. Height 3"—4".

humilis 'Violacea Black Base'
Purplish red with a distinctive
greenish black basal blotch and
yellow margins. Early-mid spring.
Height 3"—4".

humilis 'Violacea Yellow Base'
Pointed, violet-purple petals with a
broad, golden yellow base. Prolific,
easy to grow. Good in pots or
window boxes. Early midspring.
Height 4"—6".

kolpakowskiana Solid buttercup-
yellow interior; red-flamed yellow
exterior; lily-shaped. Heirloom
1877. Early. Height 6"—8".

'Lady Jane' Rose petal exterior
with tiny white edge; bright white
interior. Late-midseason. Height
8"—10".

linifolia Bright signal-red inside
and out with a jet-black base;
opens wide in the sunshine; red-
edged leaves. Late-midspring.
Height 3"—4".

'Little Beauty' Reddish pink petals
with a bluish heart; very beautiful.
Midspring. Height 4"—6".

'Little Princess' Spanish orange
with red midveins; black base out-
lined with yellow. Midspring.
Height 4"—6".

maximowiczii Shrimp-red flowers
with a small, deep-blue heart seen
when it opens wide in midday sun;
leaves upright. Heirloom 1889.
Midseason. Height 3"—4".

neustruevae Small, star-shaped,
golden yellow flowers with a greenish brown band on the outer sepals.
Sweet, honey-like fragrance. From
Central Asia. Early spring. Height
3"—4".

orphanidea Coppery orange flower sporting bluish black anthers, with a yellow base. Showy, graceful. Native to Greece. Midspring. Height 4"—6".

orphanidea **'Flava'** Petals yellow with garnet-red tips and tiny green stripes; gives a bronzy effect; multi-flowered. Early-midseason. Height 8"—10".

polychroma Little white tulip with violet-tipped petals and occasional apple-green flush; large, sunny yellow heart; multi-flowered. Heirloom 1885. Very early flowering. Height 3"—4".

praestans **'Fusilier'** Vivid reddish orange, multi-flowered perennial will add a bright spot to any garden; we have seen it repeat bloom in gardens for over 20 years. Heirloom 1939. Midseason. Height 10"—12".

praestans **'Unicum'** Sport of *T. praestans* 'Fusilier'; same color flowers and growth habits but with white-edged foliage; multi-flowered; Height 10"—12".

sylvestris Florentine or woodland tulip. Sweetly fragrant, long, narrow, greenish yellow petals, and sepals that gracefully recurve. Rarely available. From Europe and Eastern Asia. Naturalizes freely where happy by both stolons and seed. Late midspring. Height 10"—14".

tarda Star-shaped tulip of white and yellow; bunch flowering. Early spring. Height 6"—8".

'Tinka' Exterior petals cardinal-red with tiny yellow stripe; when flower opens petals reveal primrose yellow. Small but tough, strong grower. Late-midseason. Height 8"—10".

urumiensis Clear yellow interior; rust, cream, and green stripes on exterior petals; multi-flowered. Heirloom 1932. Early. Height 3"—4".

whittallii Chalice-shaped, intermediate size, rich burnt orange with pointed petals. Distinct, black-eyed center. From Eastern Europe. Late midspring. Height 8"—12".

'Titty's Star' Deep greenish gold multiple flowers appear on each stem. Attention-getter. Height 4"—5".

vvedenskyi **'Tangerine Beauty'** Show-stopping soft orange/red flower; great in patio planters and fronts of borders. Midspring. Height 6"—8".

wilsoniana Deep blood-red with tiny black heart and creamy anthers; narrow, prostrate, undulating gray/green leaves. Heirloom 1902. Late. Height 4"—6".

turkestanica White petals with orange center; multi-flowering and fragrant; a great repeat bloomer in our garden. Early. Height 6"—8".

X. *Frequently Asked Questions*

Why do my tulips stay short stemmed?

It is possible that you may have purchased a short-stemmed tulip.

The bulbs did not achieve good root formation because they were planted in poor soil or where root development was difficult. They did not get enough moisture to induce good root growth, or they were planted too late and did not get a long enough cold period.

Abnormally high temperatures in the spring kept the plant from developing fully and hence the tulips bloomed with shorter stems.

Why did my tulips fail to flower in the second season in my garden?

When you receive your bulbs, the large "mother" bulbs have sufficient energy stored for the first year's display and buds are already formed. In subsequent seasons, the "daughter" bulbs must have all of the same elements of a successful growing season, in order to store enough energy to produce blooms. If they do not get enough sunlight, water, or nutrients, and if their foliage doesn't have an opportunity to mature, they will not manufacture enough sugars for the bulb to create a bloom and hence may send up only a leaf or two or a smaller flower *(see section on Culture)*.

Why did my newly planted large (12cm+) tulip bulbs fail to bloom?

Most likely the bulbs were exposed to ethylene gas from ripening fruits or rotting organic material during storage, prior to planting. The ethylene gas causes the bulb to abort (give up) its bloom, even though the bulb and plant continue to grow successfully.

Other strange, related causes of failure to bloom are exposure to high temperatures (over 80° F) and poor ventilation during the storage period.

Opposite: An example of a classic tulip, T. 'Ivory Floradale,' in the Darwinhybrid group, opens creamy yellow and matures to elegant, ivory white.

If there is not a long enough cold period after planting and before bloom (4 to 6 weeks at 40°F or below), or if there is a drought (tulips need at least ½" of water per week while growing) that causes stress, bulbs may abort their blooms.

Why do my tulips completely disappear?

Check the cultural section in this book to be sure your soil, drainage, sunlight, and ventilation are appropriate for tulips. If all of those elements are correct, and your tulips are still disappearing, then you may have the dreaded vole as residents in your garden! Voles are what we call "underground bulb monsters"; they can completely consume an entire tulip planting. If they are present, there are usually several quarter-sized holes in your garden *(see section on Pests)*.

Sources for Bulbs

While there are numerous sources from which to buy tulip bulbs, including your local garden centers, we thought it appropriate to make a list of mail order catalogue companies that specialize in tulip bulbs (some are more specialized than others). Below are several lists of retail mail order sources, separated according to how many different tulip cultivars they offer as this book goes to press.

Companies offering 200 tulip cultivars or more:

Brent and Becky's Bulbs, 7463 Heath Trail, Gloucester, VA 23061. Toll-free for catalogue requests and orders: (877) 661-2852

McClure and Zimmerman, 108 West Winnebago St., Freisland, WI 53935. Toll-free for catalogue requests and orders: (800) 374-6120

John Scheeper's, Inc., 23 Tulip Dr., Bantam, CT 06750. (860) 567-0838

Companies offering 100 cultivars or more:

K. Van Bourgondien and Sons, Box 1000, Babylon, NY 11702. (800) 622-9997

Veldheer Tulip Gardens, 12755 Quincy & US-31, Holland, MI 49424. (616) 399-1900

Wooden Shoe Bulb Co., P. O. Box 127, Mt. Angel, OR 97362. (800) 711-2006

Companies offering 50 cultivars or more:

Charles Mueller Co., 7091 N. River Road, New Hope, PA 18938. (888) 594-2852

Dutch Gardens, P. O. Box 2037, Lakewood, NJ 08701-8037. (800) 818-3861

Park Seed Co., 1 Parkton Ave., Greenwood, SC 29647. (800) 845-3369

Rosengarde, Box 1148, Mt. Vernon, WA 98273. (866) 488-5477

The Terra Ceia Farms, 3810 Terra Ceia Rd., Pantego, NC 27860. (800) 838-2852

White Flower Farm, Box 50, Litchfield, CT 06759. (800) 503-9624

Brent's bike, with a flower bucket secure in his basket, awaits the next armload of tulips for a flower arrangement.

Recommended Reading

The Classified List and International Register of Tulip Names by The Royal General Bulbgrower's Association. This is the official registration authority for more than 5600 tulip cultivar names of which about 2500 to 3000 are currently in the trade and available for sale. It provides the official name, group, hybridizer, year of introduction, color, description, and height of the tulips. A must for botanical gardens or serious gardeners who need to know tulip cultivars' correct name, division and color description. ISBN-9073350-02-6, Koninklijke Algemeene Vereeniging voor Bloembollencultuur, 1996.

Tulips by Stanley Killinback. A fine, general overview of the genus *tulipa* from an English point of view, with a section on the history and development of tulips; descriptions and photos of about 100 tulip cultivars, some no longer available; and a section on cultivation. ISBN# 1-55521-704-4, Chartwell Books, 1990.

Keukenhoff, the Dutch flower bulb grower's garden, in which displays of tulips, other flower bulbs, and perennials are replanted each year in a beautiful park setting.

Tulips, The Complete Guide to Selections and Growing by Arend Jan van Der Horst and Sam Benvie. Sections on history, usage, and growing tulips with an emphasis on Keukenhoef and Williamsburg; good color photographs of outdoor gardens and indoor arrangements. ISBN# 1-55209-198-8, Firefly Books, 1997.

Tulipa, A Photographer's Botanical by Christopher Baker and Willem Lemmers. This incredibly beautiful, large-format, full-color illustrated book is, to date, the most extensive photographic essay on the genus tulipa, with over 300 color prints of the flowers and 500 cultivars described rather technically. Little gardening information is given; not all cultivars listed and pictured are still in the trade; and some of the most popular and widely grown cultivars are not included. However, this book is a must for tulip aficionados. ISBN# 1-57965-122-4, Artisan Publishing, 1999.

Tulips by Peter Arnold. A spectacular, large-format book filled with incredibly beautiful color images of 70, mostly popular, tulip culti-vars. Unfortunately, about 10% of the images are mislabeled or are virused examples of the cultivar that do not show how flowers should appear from healthy bulbs and in a good gardening situation. ISBN# 0-02-503251-8, Macmillan Publishing Company, 1992.

TulipoMania by Mike Dash. An excellent, detailed history of the tulip from its origins in Central Asia to the boom and bust of "tulipomania" and how it affected the lives of those who were a part of that era. ISBN# 0-609-60439-2, Crown Publishers, 1999.

The Tulip, The Story of a Flower That Has Made Men Mad by Anna Pavord. At the beginning the author states, "This is not a gardening book." Instead, it is a thorough study of the chronology of tulips from 1451, when tulip cultivation is first recorded, until 1994, when Dutch growers exported two billion bulbs. It is well-illustrated with reproductions of excellent botanical prints of tulips plus a few photo-graphs. Eighty-one species tulips are described in fair detail and over 400 cultivars, many no longer in culture, are briefly described. This is a lovely and interesting book for the passionate tulip enthusiast. ISBN# 1-58234-013-7, Bloomsbury Publishing, 1999.

A Tulip Grower's Guide

Num	DIV	Name	WT	Pink	Rose	Yel	Sal	Gr	Pur	Bur
1	S.E.	Apricot Beauty		•			•			
1	S.E.	Beauty Queen		•						
1	S.E.	Christmas Marvel		•						
1	S.E.	Flair				•				
1	S.E.	Generaal de Wet								
1	S.E.	Mickey Mouse				•				
1	S.E.	Purple Prince							•	
2	D.E.	Abba								
2	D.E.	Holland Baby								
2	D.E.	Holland Ballet	•							
2	D.E.	Monsella®				•				
2	D.E.	Monte Carlo				•				
2	D.E.	Montreux®				•				
2	D.E.	Peach Blossom		•						
2	D.E.	Yellow Baby				•				
3	Tr	Attila							•	
3	Tr	Barcelona				•				
3	Tr	Blue Ribbon							•	
3	Tr	Calgary	•							
3	Tr	Couleur Cardinal								
3	Tr	Don Quichotte			•					
3	Tr	Dreaming Maid							•	
3	Tr	Dynamite								
3	Tr	Happy Family			•					
3	Tr	Hollandia								
3	Tr	Inzell	•							
3	Tr	Jan Reus								
3	Tr	Jimmy				•				
3	Tr	Leen van der Mark	•							
3	Tr	Mary Belle				•				
3	Tr	Merry-Go-Round								
3	Tr	Nairobi								
3	Tr	Negrita							•	
3	Tr	New Design		•						
3	Tr	Passionale							•	
3	Tr	Peer Gynt			•					
3	Tr	Prinses Irene							•	
3	Tr	Red Bouquet								
3	Tr	Red Present								
3	Tr	Salmon Pearl®			•	•	•			
3	Tr	Shirley	•						•	
3	Tr	Striped Bellona				•				

Red	Org	Early	Mid	Late	Short	Med	Tall
		•				•	
		•				•	
		•				•	
•		•			•		
	•	•				•	
•		•			•	•	
		•				•	
•		•			•		
•		•			•		
		•			•		
•		•			•		
		•			•		
		•				•	
		•			•		
		•			••		
			•			•	
•			•				•
			•			•	
			•		•		
•			•			•	
			•			•	
			•				•
•			•			•	
	•		•			•	
•			•			•	
			•			•	
•			•			•	
	•		•			•	
•			•			•	
•			•			•	
•			•			•	
•			•			•	
			•			•	
			•			•	
			•			•	
			•				•
	•		•			•	
•			•			•	
•			•			•	
			•			•	
			•			•	
•			•			•	

An early morning visitor to our spring garden display enjoys T. *'Carnaval de Nice.'*

Num	DIV	Name	WT	Pink	Rose	Yel	Sal	Gr	Pur	Bur
3	Tr	The Mounties®								
3	Tr	Yellow Cab®				•				
3	Tr	Yellow Present				•				
3	Tr	Yokohama				•				
4	Dh	Apeldoorn								
4	Dh	Apeldoorn's Elite				•				
4	Dh	Banja Luka				•				
4	Dh	Beauty of Apeldoorn				•				
4	Dh	Big Chief		•						
4	Dh	Burning Heart				•				
4	Dh	Come-Back								
4	Dh	Day Dream				•				
4	Dh	Garant				•				
4	Dh	Golden Apeldoorn				•				
4	Dh	Golden Oxford				•				
4	Dh	Golden Parade				•				
4	Dh	Ivory Floradale	•							
4	Dh	Ollioules	•	•						
4	Dh	Olympic Flame				•				
4	Dh	Orange Sun								
4	Dh	Oxford								
4	Dh	Parade								
4	Dh	Pink Impression®		•						
4	Dh	Silverstream	•	•	•					
4	Dh	World's Favourite				•				
5	S.L.	Big Smile				•				
5	S.L.	Blushing Lady			•	•	•			
5	S.L.	Candy Club®	•	•						
5	S.L.	Colour Spectacle				•				
5	S.L.	Cum Laude							•	
5	S.L.	Douglas Bader		•						
5	S.L.	Esther		•						
5	S.L.	Georgette				•				
5	S.L.	Kingsblood								
5	S.L.	La Courtine				•				
5	S.L.	Maureen	•							
5	S.L.	Menton			•		•			
5	S.L.	Mrs. J.T. Scheepers				•				
5	S.L.	Perestroyka		•	•					
5	S.L.	Picture		•						
5	S.L.	Pink Diamond		•						
5	S.L.	Queen of Night							•	
5	S.L.	Renown			•					
5	S.L.	Sorbet	•							

Red	Org	Early	Mid	Late	Short	Med	Tall
•			•			•	
			•		•		
			•			•	
			•			•	
•			•				•
•			•				•
•			•				•
•			•				•
			•				•
•			•				•
•			•			•	
	•		•				•
			•			•	
			•				•
			•				•
			•				•
			•				•
			•				•
•			•				•
	•		•			•	
•			•				•
•			•				•
			•				•
			•				•
•			•			•	
				•			•
				•			••
				•		•	
•				•		•	
				•		•	
				•	•		
				•		•	
•				•		•	
•				•			•
•				•			•
				•			•
				•			•
				•			••
				•		•	
				•		•	
				•			•
•				•			•
•				•			•

Leucojum aestivum's *color is a wonderful complement to Becky's favorite tulip, 'Carmine Parrot.'*

Num	DIV	Name	WT	Pink	Rose	Yel	Sal	Gr	Pur	Bur
5	S.L.	Temple of Beauty			•					
5	S.L.	Temple's Favourite			•	•				
5	S.L.	Toyota	•		•					
6	L.F.	Ballade	•						•	
6	L.F.	Ballerina				•				
6	L.F.	China Pink		•						
6	L.F.	Elegant Lady	•	•		•				
6	L.F.	Fokker Fan Fan®								
6	L.F.	Jane Packer								
6	L.F.	Mariette			•					
6	L.F.	Marilyn	•	•						
6	L.F.	Maytime							•	
6	L.F.	Mona Lisa				•				
6	L.F.	Moonshine				•				
6	L.F.	Pieter de Leur								
6	L.F.	Queen of Sheba								
6	L.F.	Red Shine								
6	L.F.	West Point				•				
6	L.F.	White Elegance	•							
6	L.F.	Yonina			•				•	
7	Fr	Blue Heron	•						•	
7	Fr	Burgundy Lace								•
7	Fr	Fancy Frills®	•		•					
7	Fr	Fringed Elegance				•				
7	Fr	Maja				•				
7	Fr	Red Wing								
7	Fr	Swan Wings	•							
8	Vir	China Town		•	•			•		
8	Vir	Esperanto			•			•		
8	Vir	Formosa				•		•		
8	Vir	Groenland			•			•		
8	Vir	Spring Green	•					•		
9	Par	Apricot Parrot			•	•	•	•		
9	Par	Black Parrot							•	•
9	Par	Blue Parrot							•	
9	Par	Carmine Parrot			•					
9	Par	Estella Rijnveld	•							
9	Par	Fantasy			•			•		
9	Par	Flaming Parrot	•			•				
9	Par	Green Wave	•		•			•		
9	Par	Weber's Parrot	•		•			•		
9	Par	White Parrot	•							
10	D.L.	Allegretto				•				
10	D.L.	Angelique		•						

Red	Org	Early	Mid	Late	Short	Med	Tall
•	•			•			••
•	•			•			••
•				•			•
			•	•		•	
•			•	•		•	
				•		•	•
				•		•	
•	•			•		•	
•				•		•	
				•		•	
				•		•	•
				•		•	•
•			•	•		•	
				•		•	
•			•			•	
•	•		•			•	
•				•			•
				•			•
				•			•
				•		•	
			•			•	
				•		•	
				•		•	
			•	•			•
			•	•		•	
•			•			•	
				•		•	
				•	•		
•			•		•		
				•		•	
				•		•	
				•		•	
			•			•	
			•			•	
			•			•	
•		•				•	
•				•			•
			•			•	
			•				•
			•			•	
				•		•	
			•			•	
•				•		•	
				•		•	

Felines are great helpers in the garden by guarding against vole infestation. This one also adds to the ambience of T. 'Apeldoorn' and T. 'Golden Apeldoorn.'

Num	DIV	Name	WT	Pink	Rose	Yel	Sal	Gr	Pur	Bur
10	D.L.	Black Hero®							•	•
10	D.L.	Blue Diamond							•	
10	D.L.	Carnaval de Nice	•							
10	D.L.	Creme Upstar	•	•		•				
10	D.L.	Lilac Perfection							•	•
10	D.L.	Maywonder		•	•					
10	D.L.	Mount Tacoma	•							
10	D.L.	Orange Princess							•	
10	D.L.	Red Princess								•
10	D.L.	Uncle Tom								•
10	D.L.	Upstar	•	•						
10	D.L.	Wirosa	•							
11	Kf	Ancilla	•	•	•					
11	Kf	Fashion			•	•			•	
11	Kf	Heart's Delight			•	•				
11	Kf	Johann Strauss	•		•					
11	Kf	Scarlet Baby								
11	Kf	Showwinner								
11	Kf	Stresa				•				
12	Fs	Easter Moon				•				
12	Fs	Flaming Purissima	•		•					
12	Fs	Juan				•				
12	Fs	Madame Lefeber								
12	Fs	Orange Emperor								
12	Fs	Purissima	•							
12	Fs	Solva			•	•				
12	Fs	Sweetheart	•			•				
12	Fs	Yellow Purissima				•				
12	Fs	Zombie			•	•				
13	Gr	Cape Cod			•	•	•			
13	Gr	Corsage		•			•			
13	Gr	Czaar Peter	•		•					
13	Gr	Donna Bella	•			•				
13	Gr	Easter Surprise				•				
13	Gr	Oratorio		•						
13	Gr	Pinocchio	•							
13	Gr	Plaisir	•			•				
13	Gr	Red Riding Hood								
13	Gr	Sweet Lady		•		•				
13	Gr	Toronto			•		•			
14	Msc	*albertii*				•				
14	Msc	*altaica*				•				
14	Msc	*bakeri* Lilac Wonder		•		•				
14	Msc	*batalinii* Apricot Jewel			•	•	•			

Red	Org	Early	Mid	Late	Short	Med	Tall
				•			•
				•		•	
•				•		•	
				•		•	
				•		•	
				•			•
				•		•	
	•		•		•		
•			•		•		
				•		•	
				•		•	
•				•	•		
		•			•		
		•			•		
•		•			•		
		•			•		
•		•			•		
•		•			•		
•		•			•		
		•	•			•	
			•			•	
	•	•	•			•	
•			•			•	
	•		•			•	
			•			•	
•	•		•			•	
			•			•	
		•	•			•	
			•		•	•	
		•			•		
	•		•		•		
•			•		•		
•			•		•		
	•		•		•		
			•		•		
•			•		•		
•			•		•		
•			•		•		
•	•		•		•		
			•		•	•	
•	•	•			•		
			•		•		
			•		•		
			•		•		

T. *'Czaar Peter' is colorful and attractive on its own, but when planted with a companion like* Anemone blanda *'White Splendor,' the visual impact is spectacular.*

Num	DIV	Name	WT	Pink	Rose	Yel	Sal	Gr	Pur	Bur
14	Msc	*batalinii* Bright Gem				•				
14	Msc	*batalinii* Bronze Charm				•				
14	Msc	*batalinii* Red Gem								
14	Msc	*biflora*	•			•				
14	Msc	*clusiana* Cynthia			•	•				
14	Msc	*clusiana* var. *chrysantha*				•				
14	Msc	*clusiana* var. *chrysantha* Tubergen's Gem				•				
14	Msc	*hageri*								
14	Msc	*hageri* Splendens								
14	Msc	*humilis*			•	•				
14	Msc	*humilis* Alba Coerulea Oculata	•						•	
14	Msc	*humilis* Eastern Star				•			•	
14	Msc	*humilis* Lilliput								
14	Msc	*humilis* Magenta Queen				•			•	•
14	Msc	*humilis* Odalisque				•			•	•
14	Msc	*humilis* Persian Pearl				•			•	
14	Msc	*humilis* Violacea Black Base								•
14	Msc	*humilis* Violacea Yellow Base				•			•	
14	Msc	*kolpakowskiana*				•				
14	Msc	Lady Jane	•							
14	Msc	*linifolia*								
14	Msc	Little Beauty			•				•	
14	Msc	Little Princess								
14	Msc	*maximowiczii*								
14	Msc	*neustruevae*				•				
14	Msc	*orphanidea*								
14	Msc	*orphanidea* Flava				•				
14	Msc	*polychroma*	•			•				
14	Msc	*praestans* Fusilier								
14	Msc	*praestans* Unicum								
14	Msc	*sylvestris*				•				
14	Msc	*tarda*	•			•				
14	Msc	Tinka				•				
14	Msc	Titty's Star				•				
14	Msc	*turkestanica*	•							
14	Msc	*urumiensis*				•	•			
14	Msc	*vvedenskyi* Tangerine Beauty								
14	Msc	*whittallii*								
14	Msc	wilsoniana								

Red	Org	Early	Mid	Late	Short	Med	Tall
			•		•		
	•		•		•		
•			•		•		
		•			•		
			•		•		
•			•		•		
•			•		•		
•			•		•		
	•		•		•		
		•			•		
			•		•		
		•			•		
•			•		•		
		•			•		
		•	•		•		
			•		•		
			•	•			•
		•	•		•		
•		•			•		
•			•	•		•	
•				•	•		
			•		•		
	•		•		•		
•			•		•		
		•			•		
	•		•		•		
	•		•		•		
		•			•		
•			•			•	
•			•			•	
				•	•		
		•			•		
•			•	•	•		
			•		•		
		•			•		
		•			•		
	•		•		•		•
	•		•	•	•		
•				•	•		

T. 'Titty's Star,' with its greenish-gold coloration and multiple flowers, attracts lots of attention even though it's only 4"— 6" tall.

USDA Plant Hardiness Zone Map

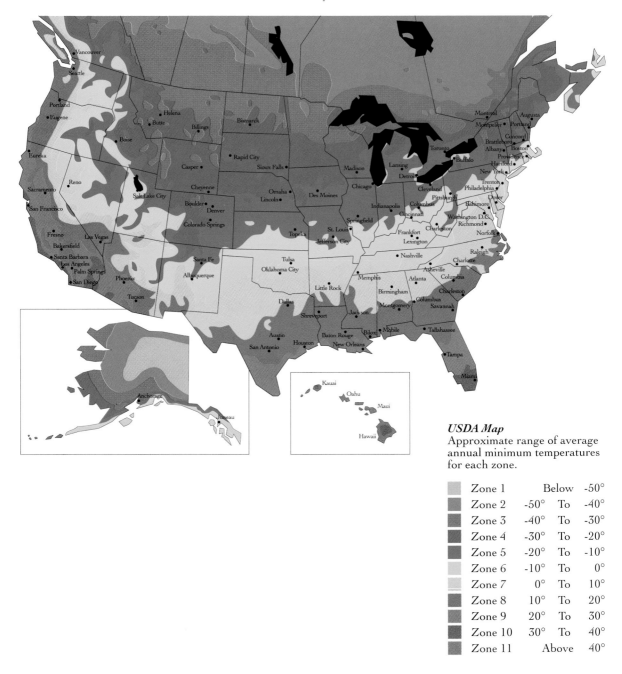

USDA Map

Approximate range of average
annual minimum temperatures
for each zone.

Zone 1	Below		-50°
Zone 2	-50°	To	-40°
Zone 3	-40°	To	-30°
Zone 4	-30°	To	-20°
Zone 5	-20°	To	-10°
Zone 6	-10°	To	0°
Zone 7	0°	To	10°
Zone 8	10°	To	20°
Zone 9	20°	To	30°
Zone 10	30°	To	40°
Zone 11	Above		40°

Acknowledgments

We've received a lot of support and encouragement from many people. Those we'd like to send a special thank you to are:

Maarten Benschop, botanist and special friend from The Netherlands, who gave us vital assistance and great help with historical information about the bulb industry.

Johann van Scheepen, for answering tons of questions about the tulip industry in The Netherlands and for his vision for the future.

We'd like to thank our son, Duke, for all his time and effort researching and compiling the data offered by North American companies. It made our work and decision-making for the tulip encyclopedia much easier.

For all the special growers in The Netherlands whose beautiful bulbs and flowers, and their performance in our gardens, inspired this book, and for all our customers who kept requesting that it be written.

Rue Judd, Vivienne Jaffe and Anne Masters, who figured out how to work around our crazy schedule so this book would meet the deadline and actually become a reality.

Our wonderful office staff, for putting up with us and our very interrupted schedule during the final editing of this book.

Index